CONTRACTION & CO

The Global Solution to C

Aubrey Meyer was born in Bradford in 1947. He grew up in South Africa and studied music at the University of Cape Town during the 1960s, from where he graduated B. Mus. in 1968 and later M. Mus. After a brief period at the Royal College of Music in London in 1970, he played as Principal Viola in the Ulster Orchestra in Belfast, the Gulbenkian Orchestra in Lisbon, the CAPAB Orchestra in Cape Town and then as a section player in the London Philharmonic Orchestra in the 1980s. Intermittently throughout this period he wrote music for various ensembles including two prize-winning orchestral ballet scores.

It was while searching for a subject for a musical in 1988 that stories of the death of the Brazilian social activist Chico Mendez led him to join the UK Green Party in 1989 and then to co-found the Global Commons Institute (GCI) in London in 1990.

He spent the next decade contributing to the policy working group of the Intergovernmental Panel on Climate Change (IPCC), and campaigning at the United Nations negotiations on climate change to win acceptance of the global ethic of 'equity and survival' and the policy framework known as 'Contraction and Convergence' (C&C). C&C is now becoming the most widely supported global framework within which to resolve policies and measures to avert dangerous climate change.

In 1998 he won the Andrew Lees Memorial Award with the following citation: "Aubrey Meyer, almost single-handedly and with minimal resources, has made an extraordinary impact on the negotiations on the Climate Change Treaty, one of the most important of our time, through his campaign for a goal of equal per capita emissions, which is now the official negotiating position of many governments, and is gaining acceptance in developed and developing countries alike." In 2000 he received the Schumacher Award for the continuation of these efforts.

Schumacher Briefing No. 5

CONTRACTION & CONVERGENCE

The Global Solution to Climate Change

Aubrey Meyer

published by Green Books
for The Schumacher Society

First published in 2000
by Green Books Ltd
Foxhole, Dartington, Totnes,
Devon TQ9 6EB
www.greenbooks.co.uk
greenbooks@gn.apc.org

for The Schumacher Society
The CREATE Centre, Smeaton Road,
Bristol BS1 6XN
www.oneworld.org/schumachersoc
schumacher@gn.apc.org

© Aubrey Meyer 2000
The website of the Global Commons Institute
is at www.gci.org.uk

The right of Aubrey Meyer to be identified as
the author of this paper has been asserted by him
under the UK Copyright, Design and Patents Act 1988

Cover design by Rick Lawrence

Printed by J.W. Arrowsmith Ltd
Bristol, UK

A catalogue record for this publication is available
from the British Library

ISBN 1 870098 94 3

CONTENTS

Acknowledgements

I would like to thank the Schumacher Society, Green Books and Marion and James Wells-Bruges of R. H. Southern Trust for their commitment to publish this material, and especially to my friends Richard Douthwaite and Tony Cooper, both of whom helped to nurture its substance over many years.

Over the last decade many people have helped in varied ways to support and advise me, GCI and/or the campaign for 'Contraction & Convergence'. Many, but not all of these, are listed below. In my somewhat relentless attempt to do justice to the argument, I have often failed to justice to them. I regret this. But I am indebted to all for the diverse help provided, especially to those who coped at close quarters.

In alphabetical order: John Adams, UCL, UK, Anil Agarwal, CSE, India; Grace Akumu, CAN, Africa; Titus Alexander, Charter 99, UK; Janet Alty, Green Party, UK; Jim Berreen, GCI; Marcel Beurk, RIVM, Holland; Ciao Biming, China Meteorological Service; John Bond, formerly GLOBE, USA; Richard Bradley, US Energy Department; Dave Bradney GCI; John Broad, GCT, UK; Ingrid Broad, UK; Colin Campbell, formerly Petroconsultants, Geneva; David Chaytor, GLOBE, UK; Lewis Cleverdon, GCI; Alberto Di Fazio, GDI, Rome; Andrew Dlugolecki, CGNU, UK; John Elford, Green Books; Paul Ekins, Forum for the Future; Robert Engelmann, Population Action, USA; Jeremy Faull, Ecological Foundation, UK; Sam Ferrer, Green Forum, Philippines; Herbie Girardet, Schumacher Society, UK; Teddy Goldsmith, Ecological Foundation; John Gordon, formerly of GERC, UK; Stephans Grove, GLOBE, S. Africa; John Gummer MP, UK; Jesper Gundermann, Danish Energy Agency; Nick Hildyard, Corner House, UK; Mayer Hillman, PSI, UK; Olav Hohmeyer, formerly of ZEW, Germany; Paul Hohnen, Greenpeace International; Jennie Holland, Labour Party, UK; John Houghton, IPCC WG1, UK; Daniel Kammen,

ERG Berkeley, USA; Rungano Karamanzira, Energy Ministry, Zimbabwe; Alex Kirby, BBC, UK; John Kilani, Chamber of Mines, S. Africa; Geoffrey Lean, journalist, UK; Ulrich and Francesca Loenig, formerly Centre for Human Ecology, Scotland; Jonathon Loh, WWF, Geneva; Larry Lohmann, Corner House, UK; Abdullah Majiid, Meteorological Service, Maldives; Ian Marks, Aim Foundation, UK; Ehsan Masood, formerly *Nature* magazine, UK; Ben Matthews, UEA, UK; Patrick McCully, Int. River Network, USA; Lynda McDonald, GCT, UK; Frances McGuire, FOE, UK; Michael Meacher, Environment Minister, UK; John Mead; Luis Meira Filho, Space Agency, Brazil; Helen Mendoza, Haribon Foundation, Philippines; Norma Meyer; Georgia Meyer; Adil Najam, Dept of Int. Relations, Boston Univ., USA; Kamal Nath, former Environment Minister, India; William Nordhaus, Yale, USA; Reggie Norton, Artists for Guatemala, UK; Tim O'Riordan, University of East Anglia; David Pearce, UCL, UK; Fred Pearce, *New Scientist*, UK; Philippe Pernstich, Siemens, UK; Danny Reifsnyder, formerly of State Department, USA; Wolfgang Sachs, Wuppertal Inst, Germany; Julian Salt, BRE, UK; Agus Sari, Pelangi, Indonesia; Nicholas Schoon, RCEP, UK; Anandi Sharan Dasag, Switzerland; Vijai Sharma, Environment Dept, India; Richard Sherman, CAN, S. Africa; Andrew Simms, NEF, UK; Youba Sokona, ENDA, Senegal; Saifuddin Soz, former Environment Minister, India; Philippe Spappens, FOE, Holland; Tom Spencer, Counterpart Europe; Hans Taselaar, INZET, Holland; Saleem Ul Huq, BCAS, Bangladesh; John Vidal, *The Guardian*, UK; Nicholas Von Glahn, SHE Group, UK; Ernst Von Weizsacker, Wuppertal Inst, Germany; John Whiting, October Sound, UK; Zhukong Zhong, formerly Foreign Affairs Department, China.

Foreword

by James Bruges

No one knows what is going to happen to the world's climate. We know that it is being affected by greenhouse gas emission from buildings, vehicles, industry and industrial agriculture. We know that the level of carbon dioxide in the atmosphere is now greater than experienced in previous interglacial periods, and that it will soon be greater than experienced in the last forty million years. The Royal Commission on Environmental Pollution reported recently: 'There is no precedent in recent geological history to help us understand precisely what consequences will follow . . . the speed at which the carbon dioxide concentration is changing appears to be unparalleled in geological history'. However, the increase in hurricanes and cyclones, the drought in Ethiopia and the floods in Venezuela, Mozambique and Orissa, are consistent with predictions made at the Rio Earth Summit in 1992. We can expect similar disasters to increase in frequency and scale.

Contraction & Convergence is a mechanism for getting global agreement on the reduction of greenhouse gas emissions. Like all the best ideas, it is easy to grasp. It is founded on two fundamental principles that cannot be questioned except by very devious linguistic distortions: first, that the global emission of greenhouse gases must be progressively reduced; secondly, that global governance must be based on justice and fairness.

Under the second principle, the emission of greenhouse gases must be based on an equal per capita allowance. It is this second principle that makes it particularly relevant to recent clashes between Civil Society and the world financial organisations—the World Bank, the International Monetary Fund and the World Trade Organisation.

In dealing with the global economy the IMF, rightly, sees the need for 'structural adjustments'. By this, it means adjustments to the economy and practices of nations that will lead to continuing, rather than short term, benefit. But the structural adjustments being imposed by the IMF on poor nations are primarily designed to strengthen the global economy in the hope that wealth will trickle down from the wealthy to the poor. Seen from the perspective of poor countries, 'structural adjustments' need to be made to the practices of the industrial nations since it is their consumption and emissions that are destroying the natural world, and it is their economic system that has led to such massive inequality. Contraction & Convergence is such an adjustment.

Contraction & Convergence is a mechanism by which money would flow from rich to poor nations as of right, not as aid. It would introduce a mechanism by which the world economy would move in the direction of greater equality. It is based on a simple principle of justice that any schoolchild can understand, and therefore should be difficult for negotiators to pervert.

Contraction & Convergence has been adopted as the basis for future negotiations by India, China and many of the African countries. In June this year, the Royal Commission on Environmental Pollution said that, 'the UK should be prepared to accept the contraction & convergence principle as the basis for international agreement on greenhouse gas emissions'.

In spite of being endorsed by governments representing the majority of the world's population, Contraction & Convergence has never formed the subject of a book. The Schumacher Society is therefore proud to have invited Aubrey Meyer of the Global Commons Institute, which developed the idea, to prepare this Briefing.

Bristol
September 2000

James Bruges is an architect and writer on issues of sustainability.

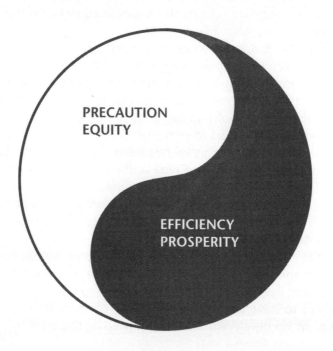

PRECAUTION
EQUITY

EFFICIENCY
PROSPERITY

Climate Change in the Light of
the Four Noble Truths of Buddhism

1. There is a problem
Global climate change is a global problem.

2. There is a cause of the problem
Systemically driven over-consumption and inequality are the cause of the problem.

3. The problem can be overcome
A global solution is needed to overcome the global problem.

4. There is a way to overcome the problem
A global framework for 'Contraction & Convergence', structured on:

    • One: Precaution
    Global contraction of carbon emissions

    • Two: Equity
    Global convergence to equal per capita shares of this contraction

    • Three: Efficiency
    Global emissions trading of these shares to ease transition costs to:

    • Four: Prosperity by other means
    Zero-emissions life-style and techniques

As the Tao says: 'From one comes two, from two comes three,
and from three come the ten thousand things.'

Author's Note

I've never been anything other than a musician. How I ended up devising a global policy concept at UN climate negotiations for the last ten years is still a bit of a mystery to me. But a clue is that both writing and playing music are largely about wholeness and the principled distribution of 'effort' or practice. Responding to the climate challenge seems much like writing or playing music, where balance on the axes of reason and feeling, time and space, can only come from internal consistency. If practice is unprincipled there is no coordination and there is discord. When it is principled, there is balance, harmony and union. Perhaps all life aspires to the condition of music.

Ten years ago, I was feeling crushed and frightened by the realisation that humanity's pollution was destroying the future by changing the global climate. A sympathetic friend told me I wasn't being 'Zen' enough. I didn't know what he meant, had a good laugh and then decided he must be right.

So I went to the UN just as the negotiations began to create the Climate Convention. There I discovered tensions between Taoists, Marxists, economists, musicians and other human beings. This was only just funny enough, often enough, to rescue me from the powerlessness and despair that otherwise captures those who are not being Zen enough at the UN, or anywhere else. 'Being Zen' probably means caring, but enough to grasp reality by letting go of 'duality'.

The 'equity and survival' case I argued at the UN tries to express this through 'Contraction & Convergence'. This starts from the oneness of the global picture and creates a framework with subdivision by principle. The precautionary principle is about survival. It says we have to unite in order to try and prevent damage and death from dangerous climate changes. This recognises the singular purpose or 'one-ness'. That is the Convention's 'objective'. That is why humanity created it. The equity principle says this must be fair across time and space between people in very different situations. This recognises 'two-ness' and shows the need to keep the feedback between ourselves and the earth in balance. It also recognises that the practice that flows from these principles of responsibility, must be flexible and responsive rather than rigid. This is the 'three-ness' but is only a product of the responsibilities and the rights created by oneness and twoness. And then, and only then, come the 'ten thousand things' of prosperity in the traditional goals of life, health and happiness with harmony in all these because we have united to prevent damage and do no harm.

So C&C is a globalization of consciousness and creates an internally consistent view of what has happened and what needs to be done. It is a framework for organizing our efforts to prevent global death and damage costs from climate changes rising out of control. This reflects the UN Convention. However, when we have failed to unite around these principles and pursue instead analysis of the 'costs and benefits' amid the noise of the 'ten thousand things', a divisive, almost paranoid, picture emerges, which ends up with the randomness of unresolved quarrels and guesswork. Working this way is dangerous, because the singular purpose of preventing the pollution that is driving destructive climate changes remains obscured by the continuing random priorities of private wealth creation. The Kyoto Protocol to the Convention reflects this directionless cost/benefit approach. This tension between the one and the many is at the heart of the global policy quarrel.

The effort recalled in this Briefing has been about resolving the tension between this one overriding purpose of damage prevention and the 'ten thousand protests' it has raised. It has been about transforming the friction between guesswork and framework back to this purpose of damage prevention.

While I hope this Briefing will appeal to the hearts and minds of a wide range of people, writing about C&C for a potentially diverse readership has been difficult. This is because, although we are all in the same boat in relation to climate change, we live in and see very different parts of it. Try addressing an audience made up of the anxious, the agnostic, sybarites and overworked mothers. Then there's academia, 'policy makers' and bureaucracy. How do you persuade them, and especially the economists among them, about anything, let alone the logic of global equity in climate policy, or the need to let go of guesswork? With honourable exceptions, those in a position to develop a response to the threat have chosen to remain captive to the very forces that now threaten us. Rather than seeking to calm the global climate, they have sought to calm us instead with mere economic management dogma. And while some of these have preened and quibbled, islands are threatened by rising seas and more and more people die from droughts, floods and other extreme events.

If this makes you just want to run away, I do too. But where do we go? Al Gore says to solve the problem we have to 'step out of the box'. But once again, step out into what? If this Briefing succeeds in making the case for C&C, staying means joining the effort for equity and survival. Both morally and logically, equity simply won't be unglued from survival and survival from equity. As in a marriage, the two are one. In fact, you can look at the UN climate negotiations as just a little haggle over an ante-nuptial contract in the shot-gun marriage that climate change forces on us all.

We have seen the future. We have the idea. We have to make an effective deal. If the right framework is adopted there can be a new growth of economic opportunity where prosperity is achieved by greener means for greener ends. This will necessarily involve all sorts of guesswork . . . but within a framework that keeps us secure.

As another expression of Indian philosophy (the *Yoga Sutras* of Patanjali) says, 'Heyam duhkam anagatam'.

The pain that has not yet come can be avoided.

Aubrey Meyer
October 2000

Introduction & Summary

This briefing is about the dangers presented by global warming. It explains how they arose, what the international community is doing about them and how humankind might, just possibly, head the worst of the dangers off.

In particular, the briefing is about the Contraction & Convergence approach to limiting the emissions to the atmosphere of the man-made gases that are causing the warming, the so-called greenhouse gases, or, as we will often call them here, ghgs. It concentrates on this approach because, in my view, C&C is the only proposal under serious discussion at present that stands any chance of uniting a majority of the nations of the world, rich and poor, behind a determined attempt to avert catastrophic climate change.

The gases causing the problem and their sources are shown in the table on the following page. The essential feature to note is that with two exceptions I'll discuss in the first chapter, all their emissions are directly or indirectly due to the use of fossil fuel. Certainly, if humankind reduced its use of coal, gas and oil, the warming effect we are having on our planet would fall accordingly. For simplicity, this Briefing will deal with all fossil-fuel-based greenhouse gas emissions in terms of the main gas, carbon dioxide. Limit CO_2, and you limit them all. If this approach turns out to be a little rough-and-ready when actually applied, we can always use the same principles to deal with the other gases later on.

The seriousness of the climate crisis is now almost universally recognised. Notes of alarm, if not panic, have been creeping into statements by normally staid and cautious politicians, officials, businesspeople and scientists. For example, the heads of the US National Ocean Atmosphere Administration and the UK Meteorological Office stated in a joint letter in the London *Independent* newspaper late in 1999 that 'we are in a critical situation and must act soon.' Six weeks previously, Michael Meacher, the UK Environment Minister had told the Royal Geological Society that, 'the future of our planet, our civilisation and our survival as a human species . . . may well depend on [our responding to the climate crisis by] fusing the disciplines of politics and science within a single coherent system.'

The Guilty Gases

Carbon dioxide, CO_2, the main greenhouse gas. It is produced by the burning of fossil fuels and changes in land use such as the clearance of forests, which cause less carbon to be tied up in the soil and vegetation. Its concentration in the atmosphere has risen from 285 parts per million in 1850 to 365ppm in 2000, a 28% rise. The warming effect of this increase is 1.4 watts per square metre of the Earth's surface. (1 watt is the amount of heat given off by a typical Christmas tree light). This heating is partially offset by the sulphates released when fossil fuel is burned which have a cooling effect. The sulphates are responsible for acid rain and if the rate at which they are emitted is reduced as fossil fuel consumption falls, the underlying heating effect of the accumulation of CO_2 in the atmosphere will become apparent.

Methane, CH_4, is a much more potent greenhouse gas than CO_2 and its concentration in the atmosphere has grown from 800ppb in 1850 to 1700ppb today, a 112% rise. This accumulation has half the heating effect of the accumulated CO_2. Methane breaks down in the atmosphere relatively quickly into CO_2 and water vapour. One third of it comes from natural sources such as swamps, paddy fields, rubbish dumps and cattle farts, the rest from coalmines and the oil and gas industry.

CFCs, chlorofluorocarbons, the main gases which are destroying the ozone layer, are powerful greenhouse gases, and their accumulation in the atmosphere currently has a quarter of the heating effect of the CO_2 accumulation although a third of this is offset by the amount of high-level ozone they have destroyed, because ozone itself is a greenhouse gas. Emissions of CFCs are already controlled under the Montreal Protocol and their levels in the atmosphere can be expected to fall slowly.

Low-level ozone, O_3, the joint creation of vehicle fumes and sunlight, contributes almost as much to the warming effect as do the CFCs.

Nitrous Oxide, N_2O, is a by-product of nitrogenous fertiliser use, the burning of fossil and biomass fuels, and the conversion of land to agriculture. It currently contributes a tenth of the heating effect from the accumulated CO_2.

Black carbon particulates, tiny specks of soot from vehicle exhausts, chimneys and all types of fire, reduce the amount of sunlight reflected back into space by clouds, and thus contribute to global warming.

Even top businesspeople are getting anxious. At the World Economic Forum in Davos in January 2000, the heads of a thousand companies agreed to a statement that averting climate change was the greatest challenge facing the world. Why had more not been done to head off what the statement called 'these devastating trends'? Note the phrase. We'll use it again. Their concern was not misplaced. According to the insurance industry, economic losses from natural disasters are currently growing at 10% a year and will exceed the projected total value of all human production within two generations if they continue at this rate. Some insurance companies have already ceased offering storm and flood cover in response to the situation, but not all can do so without destroying their other businesses like the investment of pension funds. How safe is an investment in prime city-centre property if you can't get insurance against it being damaged by a storm?

This Briefing tells a little of the story of how to recognise and deal with these 'devastating trends', but as seen from the perspective of the Global Commons Institute (GCI), a little organisation I set up with three friends from the British Green Party in 1990. My colleagues were Jim Berreen, a behavioural ecologist, Dave Bradney, a science journalist, and Tony Cooper, an I.T. specialist. From the outset we all agreed that equity—by which we meant equal rights to the use of the limited amount of the resources of the global commons that is consistent with sustainability—was necessary for human survival and should be adopted under the precautionary principle. The story is told from GCI's point of view, and the confused sub-plots usually emphasized in the official account of the decade gone by are somewhat ignored. Particularly from 1993 forward, the process lost its way because it lost the plot. As it now begins to face back towards the reality of equity and survival, the logic of equity and survival is much clearer to all concerned.

We presented talks on this thesis—as some of us put it, 'equity is survival'—over and over again during the debate around the UN Climate negotiations, and our argument and its presentation matured and improved as the decade unfolded. By the Earth Summit in Rio in 1992, the objective of the United Nations Framework Convention on Climate Change (UNFCCC) was agreed as stabilising greenhouse gas concentrations in the atmosphere at a safe value. In other words, it was a step towards survival in face of a potential climate catastrophe. The principles on which it is based are precaution and equity. I do not know how much responsibility GCI can claim for this result but we certainly helped.

Between 1993 and 1995, GCI successfully fought down the economists who had reacted against the 'equity and survival' thesis with the antithesis 'efficiency and no regrets'. This placed no value on equity and rejected the idea that there were limits. Essentially these economists wanted to proceed with business-as-usual and to navigate by cost/benefit analysis. Their argument was that equity was at best a 'normative' and subsidiary 'welfare consideration' that inhibited efficiency. They said that decisions on whether or not to arrest climate change should be made 'efficiently' using 'Global Cost/Benefit Analysis' (G-CBA). For them, as the father of G-CBA, William Nordhaus, put it, the question was 'to slow or not to slow?' This phrase reveals the breathtaking attempt to repudiate the evidence of the climate scientists and the emerging global will to adopt precautionary measures as expressed by the ratification of the UNFCCC itself. Eventually, when their methods proved that it was too expensive to save the planet, the synthesis articulated by GCI— Contraction & Convergence—emerged so as to become part of the UN negotiating process itself. In fact, we could say that UNFCCC stands for United Nations Framework Convention for Contraction & Convergence as there is no other way to resolve the argument. The only ones who came close were the USA with the Byrd Hagel Resolution.

As the climate crisis worsens, an increasing number of people are coming to realise that efficiency and prosperity can now only have meaning to the extent they are based on precaution and equity, and not in spite of them—precisely as is defined in the C&C programme. As mentioned towards the end, many eminent people have now gone on record affirming GCI's central role helping to create an international consensus around this realisation. Economics cannot be put it to work to save the planet without a framework within which to operate. Although some economists seem to think so, adopting such a framework will not mean the end of civilisation. But failing to do so will.

So what is Contraction & Convergence, and how might it help

slow, or even halt, the warming process that is making people so concerned? Essentially, it has three steps:

1. An international agreement is reached on how much further the level of carbon dioxide (CO_2) in the atmosphere can be allowed to rise before the changes in climate it produces become totally unacceptable. Fixing this target level is very difficult, particularly as concentrations are too high already.

2. Once the ultimate overall limit to CO_2 concentrations as been agreed, it is a simple matter to use an estimate of the proportion of the gas released which is retained in the atmosphere to work out how quickly we need to cut back on current global emissions in order to reach the target. This cutting back is the Contraction part of Contraction & Convergence.

3. Once we know by what percentage the world has to cut its CO_2 emissions each year to hit the concentration target, we have to decide how to allocate the fossil fuel consumption that those emissions represent.

The C&C approach says that the right to emit carbon dioxide is a human right that should be allocated on an equal basis to all of humankind. This might appeal to a majority of the countries of the world, but the over-consuming countries would have to be allowed an adjustment period in which to bring their emissions down before the Convergence on the universal level.

Some say it should be left to the market. If it were, we would effectively allow the industrialized nations, which have caused the warming problem and have become rich through their overuse of fossil fuel, to continue to use the lion's share. The Americans have proposed that all countries should cut back by the same percentage. This proposal would, of course, mean that those countries which use most fossil fuel now would continue to use most in the future. That would scarcely command worldwide support.

Withe C&C approach, after convergence each country would receive the same allocation of CO_2 emissions permits per head of its population at some agreed base year. However, during the whole process, those countries which were unable to live within their allocation would be able to buy more permits from countries which ran their economies in a more energy-frugal way. This feature would lead to a steady flow of purchasing power from countries that have used fossil energy to become rich to those still struggling to break out of poverty. C&C would thus not only shrink the gap between rich and poor but also encourage the South to develop along a low-fossil-energy path.

The equality-of-access-to-emissions-rights aspect of C&C is not there for idealistic reasons. It is pure pragmatism. It is the only approach likely to have any chance of success. And since the world has no other option apart from trying to muddle through, it is picking up wide support. Svend Auken, the Danish Environment Minister, believes that C&C 'secures a regime that would allow all nations to join efforts to protect our global commons from being over-exploited, without the risk that any country would be deprived of its fair long-term share of the common environmental emission space.' His Dutch counterpart, Jan Pronk, calls it the 'most equitable approach . . . cheaper and easier . . . allowing us to stay below the 2-degree global temperature increase.'

Some UK government ministers already support C&C, and the Royal Commission on Environmental Pollution has advised the government as a whole, 'to press for a future global climate agreement based on the 'Contraction & Convergence' approach combined with international trading in emission permits (as) together, these offer the best long-term prospect of securing equity, economy and international consensus.' If you are persuaded by the argument herein, you can encourage ministers to work for the worldwide adoption of Contraction & Convergence by co-signing the letter to them on page 91.

Aubrey Meyer
London
October 2000

Chapter 1

How the Climate Crisis Developed

The Antarctic ice tells the tale well. Samples of the air trapped in cores recovered from drill holes show that the concentration of CO_2 in the Earth's atmosphere has varied between 180 and 280 parts per million by volume (ppmv) over the past half a million years. The cores can tell us about the way temperatures changed too, and an analysis of the proportions of the oxygen isotopes O_{18} and O_{16} in the trapped air shows that local temperature rose and fell in a pattern that consistently corresponds with the rise and fall of the CO_2 concentration.*

This does not mean that temperature simply 'followed' CO_2 levels up and down. For one thing, we don't know the direction of causation—it might have been that temperature rose and CO_2 followed it rather than the other way about. Equally, it might have been that some other factor or factors influenced the rise and fall of both temperature and CO_2 levels: other factors were certainly involved. However, the cores show an undeniable but not necessarily exclusive link between temperature and CO_2 levels.

It would have been surprising had they shown anything else, because the existence of the link between the two is totally non-controversial. It is a matter of simple physics, and even those who argue that the global warming we have experienced so far is nothing to worry about accept that if emissions go on increasing, concentrations of greenhouse gases must reach the point where they have a dangerous warming effect.

The common feature about all greenhouse gases is that they are opaque to particular frequencies of infrared light—radiant heat—and prevent it being radiated off into outer space. This helps to keep our planet warm. Indeed, without this effect, we would not be here.

---

* Because oxygen-18 evaporates less readily and condense more readily than oxygen-16, the air contains less of it in cooler periods.

However, because human activities have increased the level of ghgs in the atmosphere above their natural level, they have increased the opacity of the sky to radiant heat. Solar radiation arrives as ultra-violet and visible light, frequencies not affected by the ghgs, and heat the Earth's surface. This then gives out lower-frequency infrared radiation that is blocked by the ghgs from escaping into space. Instead, it excites the ghg molecules, thus warming the atmosphere and raising global temperature above what it would otherwise be.

Increasingly rapid rates of fossil fuel burning since industrialization began 200 years ago have caused CO_2 and other greenhouse gases to be pumped into the global atmosphere as 'waste' at such a high rate that the natural re-absorption and breakdown systems have been unable to cope. The normal equilibrium between the sources of the gases and the 'sinks' which absorb them or break them down has broken down As a result, CO_2 levels are now 30% higher than any time registered in the ice-core records and are rising fast. Indeed, the surprising and frightening thing about atmospheric pollution is how recently and rapidly it has come about. There is nothing equivalent in the ice-core record. As late as 1960 we had added only 20 per cent to the pre-industrial level of CO_2, but we will be 100 per cent above it as early as 2030 if fossil fuel consumption continues to grow at its present rate. The published literature

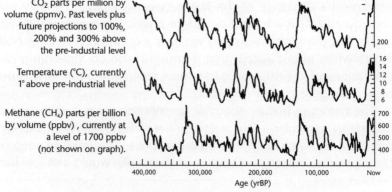

CO$_2$ parts per million by volume (ppmv). Past levels plus future projections to 100%, 200% and 300% above the pre-industrial level

Temperature (°C), currently 1° above pre-industrial level

Methane (CH$_4$) parts per billion by volume (ppbv) , currently at a level of 1700 ppbv (not shown on graph).

Correlation between atmospheric CO_2, CH_4 concentrations
and temperature over the last 440,000 years

includes projections up to 200% and even 300% above preindustrial atmospheric CO_2 concentration, with temperature trends rising inexorably in consequence (see chart opposite).

Most scientists and informed observers now regard the links between these rising emissions, concentrations and temperature as being completely beyond dispute and accept that the mean temperature of the planet is rising largely as a result of higher greenhouse gas concentrations. As James Hansen of NASA says, 'There should no longer be an issue about whether global warming is occurring, but what is the rate of warming, what is its practical significance, and what should be done about it.'

These questions are difficult to answer because we don't know exactly what effect this extra heat will have. What we can say, however, is that some of the effects, like a continuing rise in global temperatures, are now unavoidable. Although the extent and pace of this rise are uncertain, many climate scientists put the risks it poses as somewhere between dangerous and catastrophically dangerous. One of their fears is that, rather than changes being gradual, there will be a sudden flip to a new and quite different climate regime. In this, the worst-case scenario, the survival of all but a tiny minority of the human race comes into question.

I am not being alarmist. With the greenhouse effect, every successive study seems to produce more worrying projections than its predecessor because many of them discover powerful positive feedback mechanisms that will accelerate warming rather than slow it. One such positive feedback mechanism was disclosed in November 1998 when the British Government's Hadley Centre for Climate Prediction and Research issued a set of projections[1] that showed that if nothing was done to restrict fossil fuel consumption, the rate at which the world warmed would accelerate because some positive feedbacks kicked in. Average world land temperatures, which have risen by almost 2°C since 1900, would soar by a further 3°C over the next fifty years, the report said. This would be by far the most significant change in the global climate since the end of the last ice age.[2] This refers to temperatures on the land, which warms up more quickly than the sea. The Earth's surface temperature, which obviously includes both land and sea, has risen by just under 1°C.

The report added that this warming would not be uniform.

Increases around the poles would be much greater than at the Equator, with northern Russia, northern Canada and Greenland acquiring average temperatures some 6-8°C above their current level. Other workers have come up with similar results. The temperatures in the area from which the ice core samples were taken in Antarctica would rise by 15°C according to the Global Dynamics Institute in Rome, which based its projection on the data the cores themselves provide.

Naturally, a lot of snow and ice would melt if this happened, and the resulting water, coupled with the thermal expansion of the warming seas, would cause sea levels to rise by 21cm. Unless massive defences were built, this rise would put some 78 million people at risk of annual flooding, compared with 10 million in 1990. Indeed, this figure is almost certainly a gross underestimate because the model that produced it does not allow any increase in the number or ferocity of storms, not to mention catastrophic rates of on-land ice-decay in Antarctica, Greenland and elsewhere.

Although the warming would allow trees in the northern hemisphere to grow closer to the pole and thus take up extra carbon dioxide from the air, forests would contract elsewhere and release greenhouse gases as they rotted or burned. Quite soon, the release rate would outweigh the rate of absorption. 'Tropical forests will die back in many areas of northern Brazil. In other areas of the world, tropical grasslands will be transformed into desert or temperate grassland,' the Hadley report says. 'After 2050, as a result of vegetation dieback and change, the terrestrial land surface becomes a source of carbon releasing approximately [10 billion tonnes of CO_2 into the atmosphere each year].' Although this release rate is equivalent to a third of current emission levels and would consequently accelerate warming, the report says that the feedback 'is not yet included in climate models'.

A second positive feedback was also left out of the Hadley model because too little is known about it. Huge quantities of methane—a much more powerful greenhouse gas than CO_2—are stored on the seabed and in permafrost, the permanently frozen earth that covers at least a fifth of the planet. The gas is combined with water or ice to form a solid called methane gas hydrate. 'Rising temperatures destabilize the hydrate and cause the emission of methane,' Euan Nisbet of Royal Holloway College, University of London, writes in his book *Leaving Eden*.[3] 'One of the nightmares of climatologists is that the liberation of methane from permafrost will enhance the Arctic warming because of the greenhouse effect of the methane, and so induce further release of methane and thus increased warming, in a runaway feedback cycle.' He fears that warming will also release methane from hydrate in shallow Arctic seas. 'Any slight warming of the Arctic water will release hydrate from the sea floor sediments almost immediately,' he writes. 'The danger of a thermal runaway caused by methane release from permafrost is minor but real . . . The social implications are profound.'[4]

Several other potentially damaging feedbacks were also omitted from the Hadley study. One is that as oceans warm, they become less capable of absorbing carbon dioxide, that therefore builds up in the air more rapidly. A second is that changes in the chemistry of the upper air will affect the rate at which methane—which is relatively short-lived in the atmosphere at present—gets broken down. Taken together, these four effects can only mean that there is a significant risk that warming will spiral out of control during the next century unless greenhouse emissions are drastically reduced.

Although only 70% of the man-made warming effect is due to increases in CO_2 levels, it is convenient to treat all the warming as if it was (with two exceptions) all CO_2-related, in the sense that it is the direct or indirect result of the consumption of fossil fuels. One exception is the methane from rubbish dumps, rice paddies and cattle farts. Two things can be said about this. One is that there would probably be fewer dumps and cattle if fossil fuels were not used. The other is that the carbon in the methane they give off comes from the decay or digestion of vegetable matter rather than from fossil sources, so it is part of the natural carbon cycle and can be disregarded. True, an increase in cattle numbers or rice cultivation will lead to an increase in the rate at which methane is emitted into the atmosphere. This will cause temperatures to rise until a new equilibrium is reached between the rate at which the methane is broken down in the atmosphere and the higher release rate. As the effect is therefore a one-off, it is the fossil-fuel sources of methane that need our attention. The other exception is the CFCs. While these are already being phased out under the Montreal Protocol to protect the ozone layer, some of the chemicals being introduced to replace them have an even greater warming effect.

James Hansen, the NASA scientist I quoted just now, has recently produced a paper in which he argues that, because the combustion of fossil fuels produces aerosols which reflect incoming solar radiation back into space and these limit the warming caused by the CO_2 emitted, we should give priority to making reductions in the emissions of the other ghgs.[5] However, as the amount of CO_2 in the atmosphere grows, its heating effect will soon outweigh the cooling effect produced by the aerosols. Hansen recognises this and says his paper 'does not alter the desirability of limiting CO_2'. His point about priority is a tactical rather than a strategic one, and Contraction & Convergence is nothing if not a strategy.

Reducing the combustion of fossil fuels by the amount required to stabilise the level of ghgs in the atmosphere is no easy task, for two reasons. One is that the cuts required from industrialised countries are of the order of 80% and that the systems of production and consumption in those countries are so heavily energy-dependent that cuts of this order would require them to be totally transformed. The transport sector would be particularly harshly hit. However, given a long enough period to change systems and to develop comprehensive energy-saving programmes and replacement non-fossil sources of energy, no major problems should arise. It is just a question of will, of being prepared to give up the major subsidy that the use of fossil energy provides for our current activities at the potential cost of our future survival.

The other difficulty is much more fundamental. The graphs on pages 29 and 37, and the colour plate following page 32, show that there is a remarkably close correlation between the rate of increase in the world's use of fossil energy and the rate of global economic growth. This link between growth and CO_2 emissions presents an enormous problem, because our economic system collapses if economic growth fails to occur. As Richard Douthwaite, who has worked with GCI since its early days, puts it in *The Growth Illusion*:

> What happens in [industrial countries like] Britain or Ireland if the economy does not grow? In both countries, new investment is taking place each year: Britain devotes around 20 per cent of its GNP each year to increasing—not just maintaining—its capital stock, which is the national collection of machines, factories, roads, houses and so on. In Ireland,

the equivalent figure is 19 per cent a year. If there is no growth, it means that huge sums—in Britain almost £130,000 million in 1997—have been spent without generating any return.

The immediate effect is on industry. Firms that have borrowed from their banks or shareholders to expand, find that they have not earned anything extra to pay the additional interest or dividend they are committed to pay and that, because of international competition they cannot restore their margins by inflating their prices. The extra interest payments have to be met out of existing profits, which are consequently reduced, leaving less available for investment from retained earnings the next year. But less investment is needed anyway, since each business has underused capacity created by the current year's unproductive investment. So investment programmes for next year are cut back, causing job losses among builders, machinery suppliers, architects, lawyers and financiers. Naturally, the newly unemployed have less to spend with the businesses that supply them and chain stores, travel agents and garages are forced to make lay-offs too. And so we enter a downward spiral, with no growth leading to an actual depression, not just a year or two of marking time. In our present economic system, the choice is between growth and collapse, not growth and stability. No wonder people want growth so badly.

The fear of an economic collapse is the reason that governments work so closely with businesspeople to ensure that growth continues year after year, regardless of whether or not the increased production itself benefits the majority of the population. In fact, the evidence is that it does not, because an increasing proportion of everything produced has to be consumed by the system itself to keep it running, and thus is not available to go, at least directly, to meet people's needs or to improve the quality of their lives. Professor Herman Daly, who has argued the case for a steady-state, non-growth economy, has pointed out that conventional economic theory would lead one to expect that, at some point, the social and environmental costs of generating economic growth would exceed the benefit it brings.[6] 'I think in fact that growth in the United States now, aggregate growth, is uneconomic because it's increasing costs faster than it's increasing benefits,' he told an audience in Dublin in 1999.

If this is correct in other rich countries—and many studies show that it is[7]—then the only benefit of keeping the growth process going there is that it prevents these economies falling into severe depressions and throwing millions of people out of work. Against this, the fossil energy consumed in order to keep economic depression at bay is already altering the web of life on this planet for all time and threatens to cause a climatic disaster that could cost billions of human lives.

The amount of energy required to keep growing is huge. Professor Malcolm Slesser has shown that roughly half of all the fossil energy consumed is taken up by keeping economies expanding, despite the fact that they may be, by any objective standard, already prosperous enough.[8]

As discussed in more detail in Chapter Three, the UN set up a working group of economists in 1993 to advise the governments of the world on the extent to which they should react to global warming. How much warming was it economic to head off? When I saw the documentation for the conference at which the group was established, it was apparent that the ground rules had already been set and the Canadian secretariat had decided that the real question the economists had to answer was 'how much global warming can we stop without preventing the continuation of economic expansion?'

One of the arguments made for further growth is that it is needed to relieve global poverty, but there is abundant evidence that it is not doing anything of the sort. How could it, given that growth feeds upon itself? What happens is that a country burns more fossil energy in order to grow. This makes it richer, which in turn gives it the resources to become richer still by burning even more fuel and growing again. As Chapter Three will show, under this model, drastic patterns of expansion and divergence have emerged, with the

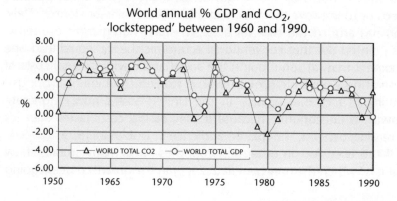

World annual % GDP and CO_2, 'lockstepped' between 1960 and 1990.

gap between the rich and poor widening both within countries and between them. In 1999, the UNDP's *Human Development Report* stated that the income gap between the fifth of the world's people living in the richest countries and the fifth in the poorest had grown from 30 to 1 in 1960, rising to 60 to 1 in 1990 and 74 to 1 in 1997. Putting this into a historical context, the gap was only 3 to 1 in 1820, before the large-scale use of fossil fuel began.

The growing inequality has been rising within countries too, particularly since 1980. China, the countries of Eastern Europe and the CIS, and OECD countries, especially Sweden, the United Kingdom and the United States have been worst affected.

GCI's position is not that growth should stop but that it should no longer be driven forward by the use of fossil fuel. It should be said time and time again, the need for carbon contraction is absolute. If the economists say that the need for economic growth is absolute too, then the need to find technologies to de-link CO_2 emissions from the rise in GDP becomes absolute as well.

GCI goes further than that, however. The increasing rate of weather damage reported by the insurance companies, as shown on the graph on the first colour page following page 32, makes it quite clear that if economic growth is to continue at all, ghg concentrations have to be stabilised rapidly. Otherwise, if damage continues to grow at its present rate of roughly 10% a year (and there is no reason why it should—given the positive feedbacks we discussed at the start of this chapter, it might accelerate), the bill will double every seven or eight years. Thus, by 2005, the damage might amount to $200 billion, and by 2012 to $400 billion. To put these huge sums into context, the value of all the goods and services produced in the world in 1997 was $20,000 billion. So a seven-year doubling rate means that by 2050 or shortly afterwards, the damage that the changes in climate do to property could equal the total value of everything that humanity produced in the course of a year.

This mid-century date is the time horizon that has caught the insurance companies' attention. However, for our purposes, the key figure is the proportion of world output ploughed back into generating growth. This is approximately 20% of everything produced, around $4,000 billion in rough terms, and as the damage bill heads towards this level from about 2025 onwards, the rate of growth will

Introduction to the Graphs overleaf:
The 'Devastating Trends' of Past and Future Climate Change

The graphs overleaf look both forward and back 200 years. They show, from the top, past and likely future projections of (1) temperature, (2) CO_2 concentrations, (3) economic growth and uninsured losses from natural disasters, 80% of which are climate related (4) the annual percentage change in industrial CO_2 emission and in GDP and (5) CO_2 emissions from fossil fuel burning split between the developed and developing country groups. As we've noted elsewhere, emissions are a proxy for income, and, at the moment, the 80% of the world's people are responsible for only 20% of the emissions and get only 20% of the world's income.

The 'devastating trends of climate change' referred to by the Chief Executive officers of 1,000 of the world's most powerful companies at the World Economic Forum in Davos in January 2000 referred primarily to the future trends of rising temperature and damage moving into the 'Business-as-Usual' curves on the right hand side of the graphics overleaf. Past fossil fuel consumption driven expansion—with the CO_2 emissions—has already moved us right out of the historical ballpark and into completely uncharted territory as far as atmospheric CO_2 concentration levels go. It is additionally the speed of the change we are triggering that is accelerating us towards disaster. To a certain extent this must now irreversibly worsen, and it is going to take a massive concerted effort globally to get out of these trends.

However, as we will argue in detail in Chapter Three, not only have these trends been emerging over most of the past two centuries (as shown on the left hand side of the graphics), but it has been during this period that the devastating trends of global economic expansion systemically forced global economic divergence as well. The international debt crisis is but one expression of this. In other words the 'expansion and divergence' and its systemic nature has already been just as devastating for the poor as the future is going to be for all of us unless—in the words of the CEOs—'more is done to avert these devastating trends'.

Inexorably, that means both the expansion and the divergence. Consequently, if we don't want a future that is experienced as the continuation of these trends—the Business-as-Usual (BAU) curves, where emission, atmospheric concentrations and temperature continue to rise out of control causing a climate catastrophe—we have no choice but to formally institute a framework of 'Contraction & Convergence' to modify these trends as soon as possible.

The alternative to the climate catastrophe is what could be expected to happen under Contraction and Convergence, where the global CO_2 emissions are cut on a planned basis and international emissions trading is allowed, to accelerate the achievement of prosperity by cleaner and greener means.

inevitably slow because the materials and energy required to generate it will be taken up restoring the houses, roads, offices and factories that the storms, floods and landslips have swept away. In other words, fossil-energy driven economic growth is likely to be forced to stop quite soon anyway. We simply don't have the option of continuing economic growth if it continues to be fossil fuel-powered.

As if this was not enough, the present system is destroying itself by destroying its markets. Poor people do not make good customers so, for as long as the polarisation of the world into rich and poor continues, sales to the less well off will shrink, and markets serving to the better-off will become increasingly competitive. This is already happening. There is excess production capacity in most manufacturing activities, and prices of items such as shoes, clothing, cars and electrical goods are falling in real terms. It has become very hard indeed to find investment projects involving making tangible goods that can offer a high return. This is partly why companies selling via the internet have generated so much stock market excitement: there were so few expansion possibilities anywhere else. So how much longer can the present mode of growth carry on?

Here again, the Contraction & Convergence approach proves to be pragmatic rather than idealistic. As the old saying goes, 'Money's like muck, no good unless it's spread.' And Contraction & Convergence would certainly spread it about by giving the energy-frugal nations emission rights to sell and by opening up markets for renewable energy technologies internationally. It would thus expand economic opportunities for everyone. It would open up possibilities rather than closing them down.

Averting the trends through 'Contraction & Convergence'

Recorded surface temperature from 1860 until 2000 shows an overall rise of 0.9°C. Future projections follow CO_2 emissions and atmospheric ghg concentrations (in ppmv—parts per million by volume). The red line shows Business-as-Usual (BAU), where the underlying emissions grow at 2%/yr. The blue line shows the lowest climate sensitivity—a total rise of 1.5°C—assuming a contraction of 60% in annual emissions by 2100.

Recorded atmospheric CO_2 concentration from 1860 until 2000 increased by 34% over pre-industrial levels. Concentrations are rising because of accumulating emissions. The future worst case is the red line as BAU. The best case sees this concentration stabilised at 70% above pre-industrial levels, due to a 60% contraction in the underlying emissions by 2100.

Damages here are the global economic losses estimated by Munich Re since 1960, for all natural disasters projected at this observed rate of increase, namely 10% a year in comparison to global \$GDP at 3%. If the global trends continue as BAU, damages will exceed GDP by 2065! The risks will soon rise beyond the capacity of the insurance industry and even governments to absorb. Damages will rise for the century ahead even with emissions contraction, but the rate can be reduced with C&C.

For the past 40 years, the global output of both CO_2 and GDP have been correlated nearly 100% ('lock-stepped'). Breaking the lockstep is essential. Future GDP is projected here at 3% a year. Future CO_2 goes to -2% with the retreat from fossil fuel dependency shown below, that limits CO_2 concentrations to 70% above pre-industrial levels, shown above. If the traded area is also converted to zero-emissions supply (below), the carbon retreat might achieve up to -4% a year.

The red line shows BAU CO_2 emissions. The solid segments show Contraction, Convergence, Allocation and Trade bringing emissions down by 60% by 2100, with an agreed 'contraction budget'. The internationally tradable shares of this budget result from convergence to equal per capital emissions by an agreed date and population base year (here 2020). If this is invested in zero-emissions technologies, risk and damages are lowered further as the budget is then net of these emissions as well. The renewables opportunity is the difference between C&C and BAU. It is worth trillions of dollars per annum—the biggest market in history.

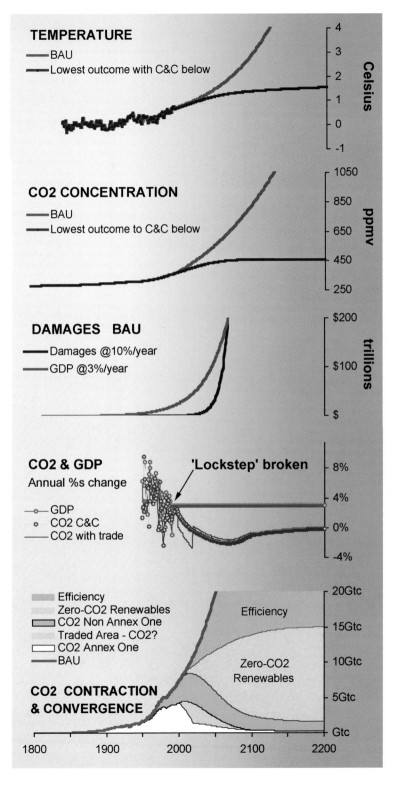

CO2 CONTRACTION for 450 ppmv &
CONVERGENCE by 2030
to globally equal per capita emissions rig[...]

280 ppmv   atmospheric concentrations of CO2 in parts per millions by volume

Temperature with 20 Year A

gigatonnes carbon from fossil fuel burning

10GT
9GT
8GT
7GT
6GT
5GT
4GT
3GT
2GT
1GT
GT

1860 1870 1880 1890 1900 1910 1920 1930 1940 1950 1960 1970

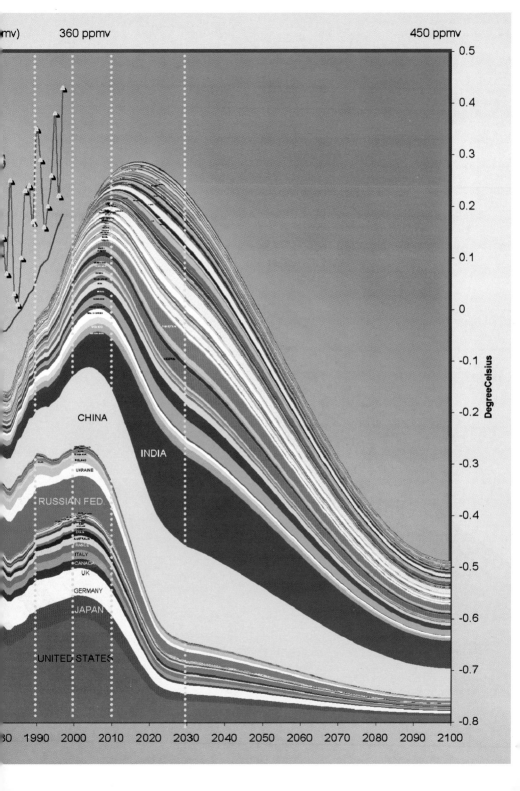

Framework . . . .

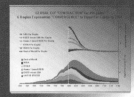

Contraction &
Convergence

Prosperity
By Other Means

GLOBAL

Inter Generational

Inter National

Needs Everyone

COOPERATION

GEO-POLITICAL
STRATEGY

Individually
Taking Chances

Randomness

Framework over Guesswork

SPACE

PRECAUTION, EQUITY

TIME

EFFICIENCY

Design

First Raise Our Growth [FROG]

Managing Risks
Collectively and
Institutionally

JAZZ
TACTICS

COMPETITION

Intra National

Needs winners & Losers

Intra Generational

LOCAL

JAZZ

FROG

Guesswork"

. . . .

Framework or Guesswork: Prioritizing the Priorities

This graphic attempts to portray visually the thought space within which the central question in this book—'framework or guesswork?' —is posed.

Our analysis is that the evidence of the 'devastating trends' of expansion, divergence and dangerous climate changes leads inexorably to the simple logic of 'equity and survival'—an internally consistent global framework for Contraction & Convergence—and that the globalisation of environmental policy now takes precedence over the fragmentary sub-global policy guesswork that is being played out in the Kyoto Protocol to the UNFCCC.

The simple timeless device of the Tao—'from one comes two, from two comes three and from three come the ten thousand things'—creates an 'architecture of understanding' for what are otherwise the random and conflicting priorities of 'Frog', 'Jazz' and 'Geo-polity':

oneness—the precautionary principle focuses on the need for a spatially unified global purpose across time and space to avoid danger which is the Convention's 'objective' (prevention by contraction), recognising that the first crucial division of oneness is into . . .

two-ness—where the principle of equity, between-ness, agreement, cooperation and togetherness (solidarity through convergence) are recognised as globally fundamental to any rational long-term (geo-political) strategy for survival and security, which does not displace but does contain and does take precedence over . . .

three-ness—efficiency, no-regrets, tactical, local, short-term, competitive behaviour with first party/second party trade-offs at the expense of third parties, 'flexibility', market-mechanisms (Jazz), adaptation, guesswork, growth and randomness (Frog), however relevant these are to the . . .

ten thousand things—the potential rewards of sustainable prosperity, because if we do not now consciously operate in what remains primarily a globally unified effort for damage prevention, our efforts will fragment further and undermine the operational conditions necessary for meaningful future choice, opportunity, mutual security and prosperity altogether.

All our priorities are now meaningful if they have been sequenced as 'precaution, equity, efficiency, prosperity', in that order; 'From one comes two, from two comes three and from three come the ten thousand things.'

Chapter 2

How the Thesis of 'Equity and Survival' Came About

The turning point of my life, the event which led to my becoming fully involved in the climate change struggle, came in June 1990 when Andy Veitch, science correspondent for Channel Four television news in Britain, broadcast a story in which he listed the five 'main offenders' in the global greenhouse gas polluters' league table as the USA, the (now former) USSR, China, India and Brazil. I was incredulous. Veitch's report was based on material from a Washington-based NGO, the World Resources Institute (WRI), so I phoned and got the WRI press releases and background information from the station. Armed with these, I co-wrote a piece with John Vidal for the environmental section of *The Guardian*, which had just been launched and which John edited. This pointed out the per capita differences of fossil consumption between these countries. At the time, one person in the US burned as much fuel as twenty people in India.

As I'd been a musician all my life, climate change was quite new to me. However, I'd grown up in South Africa, so structural inequality between rich and poor was not, and I soon realised that inequity was systematically embedded in the climate change problem. The attitudes held by rich people and powerful institutions to the world's poor were just like those of apartheid. Essentially, the rich had a policy of separate development for the poor who, *in extremis*, were expendable. This view was just as deluded globally as it was at home in South Africa. I felt challenged to generate an effective response based not just on reason but also on the strong feelings inside me. Eventually this led to the creation of GCI, as I mention in the Introduction.

In November 1989, eight months before Veitch's broadcast, Mrs Thatcher had put climate change on the world's political agenda in her 'green' speech to the UN. On the advice of Sir Crispin Tickell, the then UK ambassador to the UN, she had correctly said that humanity had begun a vast uncontrolled experiment with the Earth's climate system by loading the atmosphere with greenhouse gases. She had also asserted that the transnational corporations would be the providers of technological solutions to the problem. And, on the advice of James Lovelock and to the fury of the Greens, she had suggested that nuclear power was a necessary and viable alternative to fossil fuel burning to keep economic growth going. A few months later she told the Conservative Party conference that we couldn't all go back and live in wattle-and-daub houses as we all now lived in the great car economy.

Mrs Thatcher's UN speech and the WRI press release were part of the build-up to the Second World Climate conference in Geneva in November 1990, which I attended. On this occasion Mrs Thatcher didn't use her address to speak about preventing climate change at all. Instead, she urged the Western powers to confront Saddam Hussein who, she said, he had invaded Kuwait as part of a larger strategy to invade Saudi Arabia and gain control of the Middle East oil fields. While she moved people to war, Abdullah Majiid from the Maldives moved me to tears with his fears for the islands' future.

By the time I attended the first negotiations for what was to become the United Nations Framework Convention of Climate Change in Washington in January 1991, the Gulf War was underway, the result of Western dependence on foreign oil. The fighting caused me to make up my mind to go home and sell my violin in order to buy a computer so that I could make the case for equity and survival more effectively. When I did so, though, I felt as though I had lost a limb and acquired an artificial one, despite the fact that my electronic prosthesis allowed me to prepare attractive colour charts of every country's fossil fuel consumption very efficiently. These showed that although the average level of fossil fuel use in 1990 was one tonne of carbon per person per annum, the overwhelming majority of people in the world were way below this figure. Indeed, a majority were below 0.4 tonnes per person, the average rate that the *First Assessment Report* by the Intergovernmental Panel on Climate Change had implied was the maximum level consistent with stable ghg concentrations in the atmosphere.

The *First Assessment Report* was not a policy statement. The IPCC's climate scientists didn't say a 60% cut had to be made in emissions, and they didn't say it didn't. They merely stated that as rising concentrations in the atmosphere were due to accumulating human emissions, that was the extent by which human emissions would need to be cut to halt the rise. Even so, their statement was a bombshell in a world that was almost entirely dependent on energy sources which emitted greenhouse gas, and where the distribution of emissions closely matched the distribution of wealth. In other words, those making the money were making the mess while the rest were essentially giving the rich a subsidy. GCI published a statement to this effect in *The Guardian*, that almost 200 MPs signed. Several of the Labour MPs who did so now hold positions in government.

Despite this political support, resistance to the scientists' verdict was massive, on the grounds that it was impossible to reduce CO_2 emissions by 60%. GCI's answer was that, as most people had never reached the threshold value of 0.4 tonnes per person the first place, they didn't need to do so. The onus was on the rest of us to find a way of living on as little fossil energy as they did

Because of the CO_2/GDP lockstep (shown again in the graph opposite), a country's CO_2 emissions from fossil fuel burning are a good proxy for its national income: low income countries are low emitters. And since low-income countries lack the ability to command resources, they do not have the capacity to respond to climate change, a problem that they have not caused. This remains a major issue, as they will be hit first, and hit worst by climatic changes. While the top left-hand section of the graph shows the lock-step relationship from year to year between the percentage rate of growth of the world economy and the percentage rate of growth of the world's CO_2 emissions, the bottom left section shows how the annual flow of CO_2 into the atmosphere had built up by 1990, and who was responsible for it. It turns out to be the customary 80:20 split. The OECD countries plus the communist countries of Eastern Europe and Russia with 20% of global population released 80% of the accumulated emissions and the 80% of the world's people in the rest of the world were responsible for only 20%. The right hand side of the graph projects the flow of CO_2 forward from 1990 to 2025, on the assumption that global emissions grow at 2% per annum. The dark section at the bottom represents the amount that would have been released if the IPCC's 60% cut had been instantly implemented by everybody.

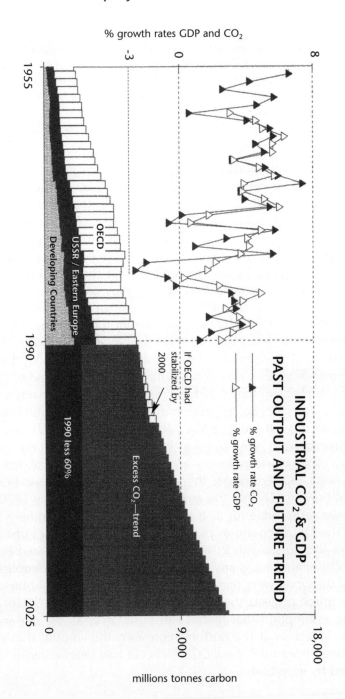

% growth rates GDP and CO₂

INDUSTRIAL CO₂ & GDP
PAST OUTPUT AND FUTURE TREND

% growth rate CO₂
% growth rate GDP

millions tonnes carbon

The Framework Convention's Key Clauses

After two years of negotiation, the UNFCCC draft text was tabled at the Earth Summit in 1992, signed and subsequently ratified. It defines the global problem and states that its global objective has to be guided by the principles of precaution and equity with a need for efficiency. Some of its key clauses are reprinted below:

The necessity for the Convention

Parties to the UNFCCC, 'acknowledge that change in the Earth's climate and its adverse effects are a common concern of humankind'. They are, 'concerned that human activities have been substantially increasing the atmospheric concentrations of greenhouse gases, that these increases enhance the natural greenhouse effect, and that this will result on average in an additional warming of the Earth's surface and atmosphere and may adversely affect natural ecosystems and humankind.' (Preamble)

The Convention's objective

The Convention 'is to achieve.. stabilization of greenhouse gas concentrations in the atmosphere at a level that would prevent dangerous anthropogenic interference with the climate system.' (Article 2) In other words, greenhouse emissions have to contract.

The Principle of Global Equity

The Parties 'should protect the climate system for the benefit of present and future generations of humankind, on the basis of equity.' (Article 3.1) They note that, 'the largest share of historical and current global emissions of greenhouse gases has originated in developed countries and that per capita emissions in developing countries are still relatively low.' (Preamble) They therefore conclude 'that in accordance with their common but differentiated responsibilities and respective capabilities the developed country Parties must take the lead in combating climate change and the adverse effects thereof' (Article 3.1), while, 'the share of global emissions originating in developing countries will grow to meet their social and development needs' (Article 3.3).' In short, the Convention covers Convergence and a system of emissions allocation.

The Precautionary Principle
The Parties 'should take precautionary measures to anticipate, prevent or minimize the causes of climate change and mitigate its adverse effects. Where there are threats of serious or irreversible damage, lack of full scientific certainty should not be used as a reason for postponing such measures . . . (Article 3.3)

Achieving global efficiency
. . . taking into account that policies and measures to deal with climate change should be cost-effective so as to ensure global benefits at lowest possible cost.' (Article 3.3)

This clause points to the global trading of emissions rights. More generally, the point to note here is that the idea of a framework based on precaution and equity had been established, with efficiency introduced in a subsidiary role purely to assist it.

Going to international negotiations armed with simple but vivid charts showing these figures worked powerfully, and eighteen months later, the Framework Convention was tabled and ratified based on 'equity' and 'differentiated responsibilities' in the light of widely differing per capita levels of world energy consumption.

Unfortunately, this advance for equity and survival was quite fragile. The US President, George Bush, refused to sign the Convention because it would have committed his country to return to 1990 emissions levels by the year 2000, a pledge he saw as being against its economic (growth) interests. So the wording of the Framework document was changed to suit him by introducing the word 'aim' into the key passage, with the result that nations were no longer committed but aiming to be committed. The British Environment Secretary, Michael Howard, was responsible for this change, which converted an emerging framework back to guesswork again. The small segments at the top of the global trend line in the graph represent the cuts the industrial countries would have been legally obliged to make under the UNFCCC had Howard not intervened. These emissions have now occurred.

Chapter 3

The Antithesis:
The Efficiency of 'No Regrets'

After the Framework Convention had been agreed, the main opposition to it can be summed up as the 'Four Noes'.

• The first was, 'No Problem', a line promoted by the fossil fuel industries and their hired academic guns who had formed the so-called Global Climate Coalition. What's all the fuss about?, these 'contrarians' asked. Climate change wasn't occurring, and if it was, a warmer climate was desirable anyway.

• The second was, 'No Regrets'. Here the argument was that action to slow down the accumulation of ghgs in the atmosphere should be restricted to things it made economic sense to do anyway. For example, it made sense to become more energy-efficient to the extent that it cut your costs and increased your profits. The advantage of this approach was that if it turned out that climate change was not happening, you wouldn't have any regrets about anything you'd done.

• The third was, 'No Solutions without Leadership'. Two environmental organisations, Greenpeace and CIEL (the Centre for International Environmental Law) argued that it was up to the countries that had caused the greenhouse problem to take the lead in combating it. They persuaded AOSIS (the Association of Small Islands States, many of whom will disappear as sea levels rise) to table radical but hopelessly one-sided demands.

• The fourth was 'No Solutions without Developing Countries'. 'What's the point of us reducing our emissions if they don't reduce theirs as well?' the industrialized countries asked, pointing out that the atmospheric concentration of greenhouse gases rose globally in response to emissions regardless of the location of the source.

As far as I was concerned, the first argument was completely bogus. John Knaess, the US principal delegate to the Second World Climate Conference put it well: the heat-trapping effect of greenhouse gases is simple sophomore physics. The higher the concentration of the gases in the atmosphere, the more heat trapped. The only questions are to do with the extent of the damage that will be done by the rising temperatures—how much will it amount to, and how soon will it start?

The second argument reflects the conflict between the need to protect the Earth's ecology on the one hand and the growth of national economies on the other. It is obvious to most people that an economy cannot grow physically for ever inside a physically limited space. But most mainstream economists think otherwise, and in 1993 they moved into the climate debate in force as part of an IPCC policy assessment programme. GCI fought them for the next two and a half years. The contest was essentially between the precautionary ecology of GCI's 'Equity and Survival' and the unlimited-stake casino game the economists called 'Efficiency with No Regrets'.

The third argument, intended as a rallying point for the environmentally correct, persisted and distorted the negotiating process to such an extent that even Greenpeace, an author of the AOSIS protocol, described its remnants in the form of the Kyoto Protocol in 1997 as 'a tragedy and a farce'. In doing this, they and the other environmentalists who had made this argument hadn't just missed the target, they had missed the point. The farce was the lack of a global framework, an outcome which they had long laboured to bring about.

The fourth argument was the point, and gave the lie to the other three. As the US correctly emphasized whenever it refused to accept proposals that involved just the industrialized world, 'global problems require global solutions'. Many NGOs and governments thought that the US was merely using this argument as a blocking tactic, since it was responsible for the highest proportion of the accumulated CO_2 in the atmosphere and was also the highest national emitter in the world. Certainly, the US did not help its own case by refusing to accept until June 1996 that human-induced climate change was a reality and that emissions abatement was therefore required.

A great deal of political energy went into the fight to make developed countries take the lead, diverting attention from the real issue of how developing countries should participate. As a result, this question did not get any real attention within the official process until much later, when developing countries themselves began to realise that their pursuit of the growth illusion would not deliver them from evil of climate change.

With progress blocked by the warming sceptics on one side, the environmentalists demanding 'leadership' on the other and the Americans playing everyone off against everyone else, the economists arrived like the cavalry and announced that the pursuit of 'efficiency' on a 'no-regrets' basis was the way ahead. GCI quickly realised that this meant turning the Convention away from precaution and equity back to the priorities of business-as-usual. The only thing that was going to be different this time would be the use of the economists' new toy: global cost/benefit analysis.

So, between 1993 and 1995 GCI dealt with the four noes as follows. We engaged in debate with the contrarians and sought debate with the environmentalists. We exposed and ridiculed the economists' approach for what it was—an attempt to re-instate growth as the world's Number One priority and oust the precautionary approach which gave its highest priority to ensuring human survival. Most importantly, we formulated a global solution to the global climate problem by synthesizing the contenders' main arguments into a compromise that we hoped would become acceptable to all sides—a trade for equity swap. In short, we turned the four noes into three yeses and one maybe.

With hindsight this all seems pretty straightforward and mundane but at the time it was difficult to find the plot, let alone lose it. Most of the time, most people saw GCI's position as some form of heresy.

Although I didn't fully understand this at first, it soon became clear that the cost/benefit tactics of the economists were intended to ensure that the issue of North/South inequity tentatively written into the Framework Convention got quickly written out. Equity was a subjective matter: in economic jargon it was value-laden and normative, whereas efficiency was allegedly value-free, positive and objective. The economists preached that, in order to get anywhere, climate negotiations had to be free of old squabbles about injustice and bolshie demands for a new, equitable international economic order. In other words, equity had to be subordinated to the 'objective' criteria of efficiency.

The problem with this was that whatever the equity/efficiency tensions might be within a single national economy, they are at least nominally subject to democratic control. Elections are held to get rid of governments that lean too far one way or the other and some sort of balance results. But the equity/efficiency tensions between the industrial North and the industrializing South are not subject to such democratic control. The Third World can't democratically vote to get rid of the First World because it is being 'too globally inequitable and unsustainable'.

The strategy the economists adopted was to get everyone to accept that economic policy tools and models of growth were not just relevant to the climate problem but the only rational means of tackling it. The tools they offered were primarily taxes on emissions and resource use, and their target was to set these at the 'optimal' level as determined by global cost-benefit analysis. That such taxes are regressive because they hit hardest at the poor was not an issue because concepts of equity were deemed irrelevant.

The economists ran into two main problems. The first was that the US was right. A global solution to the global problem of global warming was obviously necessary. The second—and this the US had yet to understand—was that global solution had to be based on international equity because otherwise the negative thesis of 'no equity no survival' came into play, with North and South indulging in mutual ecological blackmail, each saying to the other, in effect, 'I won't take my foot off the economic growth accelerator before you do too.'

The attack on efficiency

GCI fought the economists on two fronts—their ideas about efficiency and their use of global cost-benefit analysis. We used the same technique in both cases—we fought them on their own terms by extending their arguments to their logical conclusions and showing how ridiculous these were. With efficiency, we set out to expose it for what it was, a device for screening real people out of the equation in order to ensure that North/South inequity was ignored. The economists expressed efficiency in terms of an 'objective'—indeed clinical—ratio, the number of dollars-worth of national income generated for every tonne of fossil fuel burned. The higher the income per tonne, the more efficient they thought the economic system was. The problem with this is that it is self-referential. It is the economic system establishing value in its own terms. Efficiency can only be measured in terms of one's objectives and as GCI thought that the truly objective question was, 'how well does the economic system serve people and planet?' rather than 'how big can we get the economy to be?', we argued that the economists were asking the wrong question. They did this because they assumed that generating higher money incomes rather than meeting human needs was the objective of the system. So economics was not 'objective', it was *the* objective. As such it was both means and ends. It masqueraded as knowledge of both where we were and where we were all going. Heisenberg would have blushed. It made voodoo seem respectable, never mind Zen.

The dollars-generated-per-tonne-of-carbon ratio is, by its very nature, relative, as one statistic is related to the other, and GCI had to emphasise again and again that a ratio between two almost randomly moving targets could not possibly be accepted as the guide towards achieving the objective specified in the Convention: absolute carbon contraction. All efficiency can do is measure what happens as it happens. It is directionless. It is the sort of radar system that tells you after the event that you have hit an iceberg.

GCI based its response to the economists' efficiency argument on a paper we had unexpectedly been invited by the IPCC to prepare on 'The Unequal Use of the Global Commons'. The invitation had been difficult to refuse, as it described GCI as global experts on the issues of equity and climate change! The paper, which I wrote with Tony Cooper and Dave Bradney, investigated how unequal global consumption patterns had developed historically. We later called it 'Expansion and Divergence'. It showed that that high income/high emissions economies produce and consume less efficiently in terms of dollars-worth of goods and services delivered per tonne of carbon burned than do low income countries with a low emissions impact [see ideograms in box opposite]. Most people find this hard to accept, because the global 'poor' in the 'Third World' are usually characterised in the media as 'less efficient' than us—the result of a cultural bias that sees skyscrapers as 'magnificent' and 'efficient' and mud huts as dirty and inefficient.

The economists were, of course, infected by this bias in favour of skyscrapers and against mud huts. They simply did not want to talk

PRIMARY FEATURES OF THE CLIMATE ECONOMY:
Population, Production, Pollution

In the new politically guided economics of precautionary climate protection, rising temperature is stabilized. In this, however, there will still be three obvious primary features: *Population, Production* and *Pollution.*

People are measured as *Population;* Their *Production* activity measured as Income; Their greenhouse gas *Pollution* measured as Impact. These intersect each other as follows:

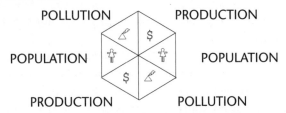

POLLUTION ⟋⟍ PRODUCTION

POPULATION ⟋⟍ POPULATION

PRODUCTION ⟍⟋ POLLUTION

Giving rise to three high/low variable scales of relationships, as follows:

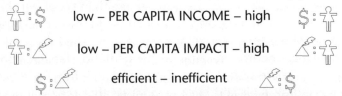

low – PER CAPITA INCOME – high

low – PER CAPITA IMPACT – high

efficient – inefficient

The detailed analysis which follows reveals
the devastating trends of inversality between:

High-income, high-impact inefficient individuals ('debitors')
Low-income, low-impact efficient individuals ('creditors')

"DEBITORS": over-consuming and living unsustainably
inefficient

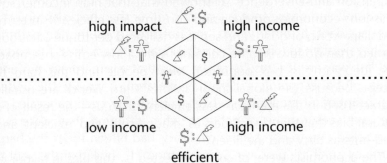

high impact   high income

low income   high income

efficient

"CREDITORS": under-consuming but living sustainably

about how inequitable it was that much of the damage to be done by climate change would be visited on people who lived in wattle and daub houses or their shantytown equivalents who had done nothing to cause the problem. Indeed, with what was risibly called 'scientific neutrality', they effectively excluded people as people altogether from their monetary assessments of the social costs of climate change. People were not people, but simply statistics. And when their work was complete, the economists were ready to write-off huge numbers of real people as easily as they might throw a sheaf of statistics into the bin.

The composite of 9 mini-graphs in the box on page 49 shows how incomes and CO_2 emissions have changed for two groups, the rich and the poor, over the past forty years. The paper I wrote with Tony and Dave sub-divided both groups into 'creditors' and 'debitors', based on the amount of carbon dioxide they emitted. A debitor puts more greenhouse gases into the atmosphere than his or her share of the amount that would *not* lead to an increase in their concentrations in the atmosphere here. A creditor emits less. We used the term 'debitor' rather than 'debtor' because, as things stand, debitors continue to debit the climate system even after they know they have exceeded their overdraft limit and have recognised that they will never be able to repay. The 'creditors', on the other hand, are effectively making a loan of their unused emissions capacity—a loan that cannot easily be recalled and essentially amounts to a subsidy to the debitors. While a debtor who doesn't repay his debts normally has his loans recalled or his security seized by his creditors, a debitor doesn't because of the structural inequality of the system.

My interpretation of the graph is that it shows convincingly that expansion and divergence is systemic rather than being an unfortunate accident. In other words, the polarised consumption patterns we have sustained (and concealed) globally since at least the end of the last war are the results of the way that a structurally dysfunctional global economic system has operated. Certainly, the under-consumption of creditors has been consistently been concealed by the over-consumption of debitors, who, although they were out-numbered two-to-one by the creditors, had fifteen times the hard-currency purchasing power. Some economists think that the debt to the rest of the world that the debitors have amassed is of no account, since it is simply 'sunk costs' or water under the bridge. Appropriate terms, don't you think, especially as the debt will cause rising sea levels and floods to submerge all the low-lying islands and coastal zones around the world?

The attack on global cost-benefit analysis

In 1993 a number of economists were invited by the IPCC to conduct an assessment of all the analyses of the costs and benefits of stopping global warming that had been done at that point. A meeting was called in Montreal to develop a workplan, so Richard Douthwaite, Anandi Sharan, Jim Berreen and I went along.

The Canadian secretariat had set the meeting up so that the problems of stopping climate change were considered in relation to the effect on economic growth. This did lead to one of the meeting's lighter moments, when a World Bank economist went to the podium to explain the Bank's PRINCE programme, so-called because its full title was the PRogramme for measuring the INcremental Costs of protecting the global Environment. Unfortunately, the prince quickly turned out to be a frog. It was already being suggested that Northern carbon polluters could seek carbon reduction credits by growing a 'carbon-absorbing' tree plantation in the South. The PRINCE argument suggested that since the South needed the trees anyway, they should only get the 'incremental cost' that covered the alleged 'global warming benefit', perhaps10% of the full price of growing the plantation.

I told the economist that this gift-wrapped nonsense wasn't the PRINCE programme, it was the KING (Keep Industrial Nations Growing) programme. There was consternation. Jim Berreen was in tears of laughter. Jim Bruce, the chairman of the session, apologised to the speaker saying that, 'he was only trying to be helpful'. The chairman of the IPCC, Bert Bolin, sought to calm the diplomats saying that, 'academics are well known for rough talk'. Then the Saudi Arabian delegate suddenly intervened saying, 'we support everything said by this NGO!' Everyone cracked up. It was only later that I discovered that the hapless economist was called Ken King!

Global cost-benefit analysis was merely another aspect of the economists' quest for efficiency, as it was intended to reveal the most cost-effective climate policy. It was, however, a worthless

The 'Devastating Trends' of Expansion and Divergence

The global average GDP dollars per tonne carbon from fossil fuel burning for the year 1990, for example, was around $3,000 per tonne. Each nation's allowable carbon usage of 0.4 tonnes per person per annum was converted into a figure called 'sustainably derived income' (SDI), by reducing this global annual average figure of $3,000 per tonne by 60%. So for 1990 while global SDI was around $1,200 per person per annum, national SDIs were obtained by multiplying that figure by each countries population for that year.

These allocations were then compared with each nation's actual dollar equivalent income (GDP) to give a 'debit' or 'credit' figure. Debit here means in any year the amount by which a nation exceeded its equitable share of SDI globally. Credit means in any year the amount by which a nation fell short of its equitable share of SDI globally. 'Debitor' means in any year the total number of people in the nations that took more than their equitable share of SDI globally. 'Creditor' means in any year the total number of people in the nations that took less than their equitable share of SDI globally.

The exercise that follows was carried out as above for each of the years 1950 to 1990, to reveal the trends. It is numerate and logical. It relies on the principle that each person has an equal right to use the atmosphere and an equal responsibility to protect it. The data used were from the US Energy Department for emissions, the UN for population, the IMF for GDP and Penn State University for PPP assessments. Production is measured in terms of US dollars adjusted for purchasing power parity, thus cleansing the data of exchange rate distortions so as to reveal the local (as opposed to the global) purchasing power of each country's currency. When data for all the population, production and pollution for all countries for all the years between 1950 and 1990 were globally analysed in this way, the picture that emerges was sustained Expansion and Divergence.

What the graphs show is the total number of countries which were 'creditors' and 'debitors' in each year; their respective gross and per capita Impacts; their respective gross and per capita Incomes in $US and $PPP; their respective Efficiency trajectories in $US and $PPP. For simplicity and anonymity each grouping of countries is aggregated and simply shown as 'creditors' and 'debitors'.

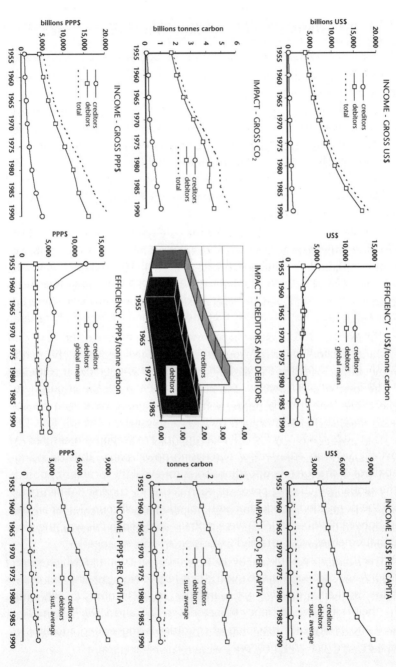

US$ INCOME QUOTAS: Creditor's and Debitors' Relative **Incomes, Impacts and Efficiencies** in US$ and PPP$, 1950-1990

The results show there was an increasing majority of $US Income *creditors* over *debitors* reaching 2:1 by 1990. (See graphic).

The gross combined CO_2 Impact of *debitors* and *creditors* (see middle graphic in left hand column) rose at over 2% a year, split between them at approximately 10:1 throughout.

The average per capita Impacts of *debitors* and *creditors* (see middle graphic in right hand column) rose throughout the period, split on average 10:1 throughout. The average per capita Impact of the *creditors* was decreasingly less than the global average.

The gross combined $US Income (see graphic in top left hand corner) of the *debitors* and the *creditors* rose across the period, split at increasingly more than 10:1 throughout.

The average per capita $US Income (see graphic top right hand corner) of debitors rose across the entire period. The average per capita $US Income of creditors remained constant overall, at increasingly less than half the value of 'sustainably derived income' (SDI). In other words, the distribution between *creditors'* and *debitors'* Income polarised significantly throughout.

The average $US Efficiency (see top graphic in middle column) of *creditors* and *debitors*, initially favouring *creditors*, reversed over the period, with debitors following the slightly rising global average towards the end of the period and *creditors* declining below the global average. This reflects the 'penalty' the poorer soft currency countries sustain through being measured in $US or hard currency equivalent.

The gross combined PPP Income (see graphic in bottom left hand corner) values of the *debitors* and the *creditors* rose on average and the less than 10:1 initial split continued throughout.

The average per capita PPP Income (see graphic bottom right hand corner) of debitors rose, while the average per capita PPP Income of *creditors* rose only to the threshold value of SDI. The split between the per capita PPP Income of *creditors* and *debitors* was less than 10:1 throughout.

The average PPP Efficiency (see bottom graphic in middle column) of *creditors* was always higher than the *debitors*. The global average rose slightly throughout the period, with debitors always just below this average. The comparison of this Efficiency measure in PPP and $US debunks the propaganda advantage claimed by Western economists who maintained that developing countries were relatively inefficient.

The combined picture—at least in PPP$—shows that the *debitors'* high per capita Income goes with high per capita Impact at low Efficiency values, and that the *creditors'* low per capita Income goes with low per capita Impact at high Efficiency values. The most striking point about this regime is that by the end of the period, two-thirds of global population are *creditors* sharing 6% of global US$ GDP, whilst the other third are *debitors* sharing 94% of global US$ GDP.

exercise because it was based on highly selective and discriminatory assumptions about the real world and the relative value of its peoples, ecological services and their general relevance to 'the economy'. Naturally, these values were all declared in dollar terms, although William Nordhaus fired off an angry fax to me saying that I could have it all in 'spotted-owl equivalents' if I preferred these to dollars.

Incredible as this still seems to me, the economists' aim was to weigh the damage costs likely to result from climate change against the costs of cutting emissions so as to prevent these damages. Why do I say incredible? Well, everything had a price and when their calculations showed that the cost of preventing climate damage was greater than the cost of the damage itself, they began advocating what was, in effect, the sale of planet to the economy.

This is no exaggeration. Indeed, there are economists about who quite openly see the economy as a sort of scorched earth preamble to off-planet solutions ahead. (As I write, Stephen Hawking has just said that global warming will force humans to move to another planet.) Intellectually, the cost-benefit analysis exercise was bathos while, at a practical level, it had the effect of delaying action on emissions reduction. In essence, it made genocide the preamble to a creeping collective suicide.

The economists effectively proved that it was too expensive (or 'inefficient') to save the planet, as the damages cost less than their prevention. One of the main reasons why the damage costs were so low in relation to the prevention costs was that the lives to be lost in the poor countries were valued at a fraction of those in the wealthy countries. Poor people vulnerable to the increase of floods and cyclones caused by the rich people's pollution were seen as less valuable than Europeans and Americans because their ability to buy the right to live* was only a fifteenth of those in countries where productivity had been boosted by the use of fossil fuel. Thus, in the surreal mindset of the cost/benefit analysts, the effective murder of members of the world's poorer populations was only a fifteenth of the consequence as the death of a member of a richer one. In its normal manner, GCI turned this around by saying that if avoiding environmental damage through emission-cuts was the purpose of the exercise, it would be fifteen times more cost-effective to shoot a single rich person with one bullet than to waste fifteen bullets on the poor. Naturally, the economists refused to discuss this; moreover they would never tell us why, if a spotted owl equalled a spotted owl, a human didn't equal a human.

The economists portrayed the prevention of further climate damage as a serious threat to economic growth because of the difficulties posed for the high-income economies by the lock-step between national incomes and greenhouse emissions. They therefore proposed that the world should seek to adapt to climate change rather than prevent it. The term 'adaptation' consequently—and quite deservedly—acquired a genocidal meaning, especially after angry articles in the Indian press.

Although the economists foresaw that the death rate from climate change was likely to rise to millions and potentially hundreds of millions over the years, their report showed that the total damage to the world economy would only be losing an 'absorbable' 1.5 % of global GDP in fifty years' time as a result of climate change. This figure is in stark contrast to the insurers' current estimates, which suggest that damages could amount to 100% of world GDP by then. On the other hand, because of the skewed approach to valuation the economists used, the cost of preventing even a part of this was seen as much higher and consequently not worth the expenditure. When questioned about how he would explain to a peasant

---

* The economists were using a CBA technique called 'Willingness to Pay' rather than the more suitable one 'Willingness to Accept' because the latter would have shown the costs of the damage to be much higher. With Willingness to Pay, economists calculate how much the person could afford to pay to save his/her life. With Willingness to Accept, they either ask the subject how much he or she would need to be compensated for their premature death or, more usually, work out a figure based on the extra that people have to be paid to get them to enter more dangerous jobs.

farmer living on the Bangladeshi delta why he was likely to lose his family, his life and his land, one of the economists, Richard Tol, declared chillingly that it was necessary to understand that, 'our analyses are carried out under conditions of anonymity'.

The economists told us the assumptions they had used, and the conclusions drawn from those assumptions, could not be questioned, as they were 'scientific'. GCI didn't accept this, of course, and although we didn't approve their techniques, we worked to show the ridiculous nature their methods and assumptions by refining them. We therefore corrected their discriminatory valuation of peoples' lives, added damage categories that had been omitted, estimated how much damage levels would rise as some climate-feedbacks had turned positive, and corrected international exchange rate distortions. Our results showed that the damage that could be done by global warming by 2050, could amount to anywhere between 1% and 130% of the world's total output in that year. We then presented these to the economists, and asked 'Is this what you meant?' Just changing one thing and applying the wealthy-country cash value of life uniformly meant that the cost of climate damage outweighed the prevention costs by a factor of twenty, making prevention the optimal strategy. Of course, it was that anyway. Any normal person readily accepts that the benefits of survival outweigh the savings to be made by adopting policies that lock the human race even more firmly into the 'devastating trends' that threaten to end it altogether.

The economists finally lost the argument when we showed that they had calculated regional damages in exchange rate adjusted amounts and then expressed these as percentages of regional GDP not so adjusted. In effect they divided apples by oranges, a fundamental mistake. It was all terribly embarrassing, as the figures had been through three full stages of international expert peer review. As a result, the economists' immoral and incompetent numbers were rejected and their methods were emphatically condemned in the grandly named 'Summaries for Policy Makers' in the IPCC's *Second Assessment Report*.

In effect, the economists were using their analytical methods to advocate business as usual. But business as usual is merely the sum of tactical guesswork in a market that has no idea of where it is going or why. After their fall, carbon taxes, the main policy instrument they had been recommending to bring carbon emissions down, fell out of favour too. Taxes are, of course, totally consistent with the business-as-usual approach, as their rates can be adjusted from time to time according to how events develop. There are, however, two major problems with them. One is that they hit the poor in any country more harshly than the rich, since the less well off spend a greater proportion of their income on buying fuel. The other is that their effectiveness varies according to the trade cycle— a tax rate that achieves its objective in limiting emissions in a period of strong economic growth will be much too harsh when that same economy is in recession.

Gradually, these problems were recognised, and the idea that an effective precautionary global climate policy consensus could be built on a system of eco-taxes which allowed the continuation of the systematic exploitation and environmental damage embedded in expansion and divergence began to appear absurd, even to some of the economists. William Nordhaus himself was moved to write:[1]

> Once we open the door to consider catastrophic changes, a whole new debate is engaged. If we do not know how human activities will affect the thin layer of life-supporting activities that gave birth to and nurture human civilization and if we cannot reliably judge how potential geophysical changes will affect civilization or the world around us, can we use the plain vanilla cost-benefit analysis (or even the premium variety in dynamic optimization models). Should we not be ultraconservative and tilt towards preserving the natural world at the expense of economic growth and development? Do we dare put human betterment before the preservation of natural systems and trust that human ingenuity will bail us out should Nature deal us a nasty hand?

Having asked the questions, he asserts a preference for the judgement of natural and social scientists over the judgement of philosophers and politicians. But he acknowledges the 'massive uncertainties' and suggests that 'coping with climate change is a worthy challenge for us all.' This is all a far cry from 'spotted owl equivalents', and his initial suggestion that climate change was of no consequence to the US as they had air conditioning and shopping malls.

In other words, people started to see the obvious. Without a reasoned framework of global emissions quotas within which to coop-

erate, eco-taxes would merely intensify conditions of mutual ecological blackmail between rich and poor. Each country would have
its foot hard on the accelerator of its screaming engine of economic growth, while all the time the exhaust gasses were heating the
planet and cooking the future goose.

The decline in support for taxes meant that quotas got more consideration. This was a big step forward, because management by
quotas is rationing. This subordinates the growth economics of efficiency and 'no regrets' to the global politics of precautionary limits
and equity. Under a quota system, a strict limit or legally binding cap
on total emissions has to be agreed. The emissions permissible under
this limit have then to be predistributed on some basis. The difference between 'pre-distribution' and redistribution is important. As
there are as yet no property rights to use the atmosphere, in order
to trade such rights they have first to be created. This is the
sequence known as cap-and-trade. Trading would certainly redis-
tribute the rights but they first need to be distributed amongst the
trading parties. This initial distribution is the 'pre-distribution'. The
logic is that you cannot trade what you do not own, and ownership
is impossible without limits.

So on what basis should the total emissions quota be predistributed, given that global agreement to the quota system is necessary for it to work? Since the world's atmosphere belongs equally to
everyone if it belongs to anyone at all, the only basis on which such
an agreement seems possible is that there must—eventually at
least—be an equal quota allocation to everyone in the world. These
are not quotas of human-created wealth. They are of wealth
received by humans from providence.

It also slowly began to sink in that a global agreement on CO_2
reductions would be impossible if it tried to protect the massive
inequalities in consumption between over-consumers and under-
consumers. The reality was that the 'debitors' would have to reduce
their emissions by even more than 60% of their current level while
the 'creditors' could be allowed to increase their emissions until both
groups' pollution levels converged. The right conditions for the
acceptance of C&C had emerged.

Chapter 4
The Synthesis:
Contraction & Convergence

After the UN Framework Convention on Climate Change had been ratified, the first conference of the signatories was held in Berlin in April 1995. Cognoscenti call this COP-1—COP is short for Conference of the Parties to the UNFCCC. There have been four other COPs since (COP-6 will take place shortly after this book appears), and Contraction & Convergence developed and won acceptance during these and other international meetings during the 1995-8 period. Here are some of the milestones.

COP-1 Berlin, April 1995
COP-1 was the meeting at which the economists' contribution to the IPCC's *Second Assessment Report* was put on trial in front of the world. The Indian government played a key role. I drafted the letter it sent to all the heads of delegations denouncing the 'absurd and discriminatory' economic methods used in the report and demanding that these must be 'purged from the process'. Kamal Nath, the Indian environment minister who had asked me to draft the letter, went on to recommend the principles of Contraction & Convergence to the conference in the following terms:

> We face the actuality of scarce resources and the increasing potential for conflict with each other over these scarce resources. The social, financial and ecological inter-relationships of equity should guide the route to global ecological recovery. Policy instruments such as tradable emissions quotas, carbon taxes and joint implementation may well serve to make matters worse unless they are properly referenced to targets and time-tables for equitable emissions reductions overall. This means devising and implementing a programme for convergence at equitable and sustainable par values for consumption on a per capita basis globally.

Nath's synthesis could have guided the world's search for a solution from that moment forward but, sadly, COP-1 was largely pro-grammed by Greenpeace and CIEL, the Centre for International Environmental Law. The two NGOs had been advising the Association of Small Island States (AOSIS), which tabled what was known as the AOSIS Protocol. This advocated 20% reductions on 1990 emissions levels by 2005 for developed countries only. The two NGOs took this position on what were essentially moral grounds, using the tiniest and most vulnerable group of countries to highlight the disasters ahead. They felt that under 'differentiated responsibili-ties' clause of the Convention, the industrialized countries had to be seen to take the lead in cutting emissions before the developing countries joined in. Moreover, in spite of successive US statements to the contrary, they believed that the US would ultimately give in to international moral pressure to make cuts unilaterally.

Despite having ratified the Framework Convention, the US again rejected the idea that only industrial country emissions should be controlled. It also continued to oppose the idea that there should be differentiated responsibilities. Instead, it wanted every country to cut back by the same percentage amount. At the end of a great battle, the meeting finally adopted the 'Berlin Mandate', which said the industrialized countries would cut their emissions again once they had carried out those they were already 'aiming' to make under the Convention.

COP-2 Geneva, June 1996

By the time COP-2 opened, most governments had accepted the judgement of the IPCC's Second Assessment Report (SAR) that there was 'discernible evidence' of human impact on the climate system. Moreover, GCI's case against the economists' methods and valua-tion techniques had been won, and although the cost-benefit pro-cedures were still in the technical part of the report, they were sav-aged in the chapter summaries written by the politicians.

Determined to focus on its suggested synthesis, the GCI team took the first billboard-size colour printouts of how all countries emissions would behave under Contraction & Convergence and dis-played them prominently on the walls of the entrance to the coffee area where delegates went for refreshments. A version of these graphs can be found in the centre of the colour pages. The interest was immense. Delegations, sometimes with their ministers, came and made favourable comments. As past emissions and future projected emissions rights could be seen all at once, everybody could see where their country was in relation to the others in the equity and survival stakes. When the US, after railing yet again in the conference hall about industrialized countries having to act while the others didn't, had declared that the AOSIS Protocol was 'unrealistic and unachievable' and rejected it out of hand, the GCI imagery showed what it would take to bring about a solution in which all nations were involved.

Any attempt to halt climate change is a dead letter without American ratification of a set of arrangements that really compel countries to control their emissions. This is because, with 4% of world population, the US is responsible for a quarter of any year's ghg output and one third of the extra amount of greenhouse gases that have built up in the atmosphere since the Industrial Revolution began. By seeking to share the responsibility for climate change and the costs of mitigating it uniformly around the world, the Americans were trying to avoid having to share the wealth they had derived from the process that had had such a serious impact on the planet. The US position was rational but unreasonable, so what was the solution to be? Rather than continuing to annoy the US by insisting that the industrial countries acted alone, a few pragmatists felt that the model of precaution and equity advocated by the Indians at COP-1 should be reconsidered as it obviously offered better prospects of American acceptance. As a result, Contraction & Convergence was re-introduced to the UN process by the fifteen English-speaking countries that make up the Africa Group.

At the end of COP-2, a man appeared at C&C billboard and exclaimed, 'Good God, a solution. Can I have that?' He turned out to be Tom Spencer MEP, who was soon to become chairman of the Conservative MEPs, and subsequently chairman of the European Parliament's Foreign Affairs Committee. He said he was president of GLOBE, the Global Legislators' Organization for a Balanced Environment. Within a year under Tom's leadership, GLOBE had convinced parliamentarians on four continents to pass resolutions backing C&C as the only way to make the Framework Convention meaningful. The European Parliament as a whole took this position from

The C&C 'Heresy'

From the global or 'top-down' perspective, C&C is the only way we can construct the deal that solves the problem with a 'goal specific' framework. Unsurprisingly, from the 'bottom-up' CBA derived perspective, this is the C&C 'heresy'.

C&C is conceived like this. The holist signal of One (contraction budget) Two (dividing up the budget through convergence) Three (distributing these equitable shares) The Ten Thousand Things (internationally trading these shares) comes down strategically and meets the noise coming up from all the reductionist behaviour of conflicting tactical assumptions in the world of money trying to construct an effective deal by an 'accident of aggregation'. This is the real heresy.

Since the rate of destroying wealth is now (according to insurance companies) three times the rate at which we create it we have to ask ourselves just how much more of this accident we can afford and whether it could ever be effective anyway? How much responsibility are we still prepared to shuffle off in what's left of the future?

I asked Tony Cooper to construct a computer model enabling all rates of Contraction & Convergence to be computed. This alone made it possible to make any computer-graphic imagery of global emissions permits rationally shared between all countries over future time. The model is a great piece of software engineering as it really can be very easily adjusted to show any rates of Contraction & Convergence in any combinations with printouts accordingly. But its organising procedures are sequenced in irreducibly simplicity.

A global total of carbon is permitted under a global contraction profile and international shares in this arise as a result of convergence from 'now' where emissions are as given (lock-step makes them broadly proportional to income), to an agreed convergence point in the future timeline after which the shares remain proportional to international populations or a base year thereof. There is not a single dollar in this basic analysis. It is just carbon and the people consuming it organised in a way that a child can understand. If the organising principles had been made more complicated, such as introducing the all-too-loaded dollars, conflicting assumptions about these results in the randomness that immediately overwhelms the basic and simple rationale. Nobody understands this, especially not adults, because it can't be done. Like music, for example, the ten thousand things in this must have organising principles based on its acoustic ingredients, before any audience applause.

What is being done in the C&C framework procedure is to logically assign international rights (these have limits and are thus less abstract than money which doesn't have limits) to use the global atmosphere on the basis of a precautionary global limit to atmospheric carbon concentration and the basis of arranging the internationally equitable shares of the global carbon consumption that is available subject to that limit. This is a rational framework.

The point is this: not only is there no other way to draw the picture on the wall, there is no other way to organise an effective global deal. If it is not done this way, proceedings are not precautionary and not globally rational, they are guesswork.

1998 onwards. Spencer left the European Parliament in 1999, now chairs Counterpart Europe, a non-profit, international, sustainable development organisation that is aggressively promoting Contraction & Convergence.

1996 saw setbacks too, of course. One of these was that several environmental NGOs came out against C&C. In some cases this was because they objected to emissions trading, which they felt might permit the over-emitting countries to buy in the emissions rights they needed and escape changing their ways of life.

Inter-Sessional meeting, Bonn, April 1997

Inter-sessional meetings are opportunities for the participants in the COP process to get together in the absence of their ministers to try to move the process on. At this one, the US formally introduced its own 'global solution', in which every country was included in the arrangements for emission control. When I read the document carefully I was delighted to discover that it was fully consistent with Contraction & Convergence for the simple reason that the Americans had deliberately omitted to quantify any of the commitments they wanted countries to make.

Deng Xiaoping had just died, and the Chinese were grumpy. The head of their delegation, Mr Zhong, gave me a drubbing, saying that the C&C graphs, which were on display and better than ever, were 'very dangerous'. This was a little rich. A year previously he had insisted that past emissions must be included in the graphs as well as future projections of emissions rights under C&C, if the Chinese were to take a positive view of this approach. His unexpected line now was, 'You are blaming us.'

I told him this was nonsense and he knew it. We could fall out over a disagreement, but not over a misunderstanding. The graphs didn't show an emissions trend prediction, they showed a projection of emissions rights. He conceded that he knew that. The problem was that his officials didn't. I told him that I would put a large note on the billboard saying, 'This is not a trend prediction, this is a projection of emissions rights.' So, each lunch break for the rest of the two weeks, Mr Zhong ate his sandwiches next to the billboard bearing the note and his officials invited me to Beijing.

Immediately before my visit to China, I went to Washington and gave a series of briefings on C&C to bodies such as the Department of Energy, the Environmental Protection Agency, the State Department and the AFLCIO. The general reaction was that the C&C model was a beautiful piece of work. In the Energy Department I was told there was only one man to reach in China but I'd never get to him and I'd be watched every step of the way. His name was Song Jian, the State Counsellor for Climate Change and Population, who was known to the Americans as the 'seven megaton gorilla' because he had his finger poised over the start button of a coal-fired development project which would lead to that amount of fossil-fuel consumption each year. If the Chinese could be persuaded to play Contraction & Convergence, they said, the US would have to play too as it would become the only game in town.

Things went well in China. I didn't get to see Dr. Song Jian, but I saw many of his officials and that October the man himself made the following statement at the closing ceremony of the China Council for International Co-operation on Environment and Development.

> When we ask the opinions of people from all circles, many people, in particular the scientists, think that the emissions control standard should be formulated on a per capita basis. According to the UN Charter, everybody is born equal, and has inalienable rights to enjoy modern technological civilization. Today, the per capita consumption is just one tenth of

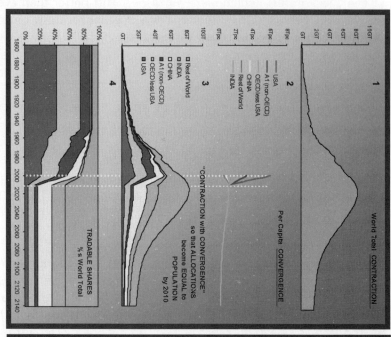

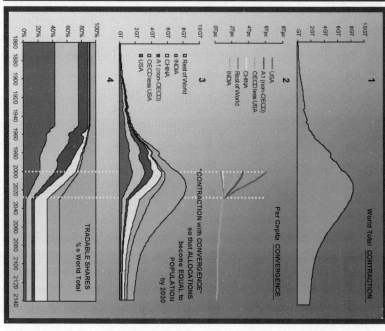

that of the developed countries, one eighth of that of medium developed countries. It is estimated 30-40 years would be needed for China to catch up with the level of medium developed countries.

Any date of convergence on equal per capita emissions can be portrayed in the C&C model. I was therefore able to adjust it to show the US reaching convergence by 2100 in one scenario, and the Chinese by 2010 in another. I showed both countries this and told them that negotiating the date (and hence the rate) of convergence was their problem not mine. The graphs opposite show two rates of convergence: one by 2030, one by 2010. A faster rate of convergence simply meant that high population, low-per-capita emissions countries like China got a larger share of emissions permits sooner. If these permits were tradable, any high-emissions country such as the US which found itself unable reduce its emissions quickly enough, could always buy the permits it would have got itself if the convergence period had been longer.

In other words, under C&C, negotiations about the date at which all nations should converge on the same per capita entitlement are only about money. And, of course, the resources that money represents. Politicians should determine the convergence rate. It will be a compromise. Economists should simply advise how best to handle the consequences after the fact.

The Byrd-Hagel Resolution, June 1997
While I was on my way to China, two US senators, Robert Byrd and Chuck Hagel, tabled a resolution in the Senate that set out their objections to the 'flawed' Berlin Mandate, and to the document then being drafted for COP-3 that eventually became the Kyoto Protocol. What started as an attempt by Senator Byrd to protect his coal miners in West Virginia grew into a broad position voted for even by GLOBE members who were alive to the dangers of climate change. Their fundamental position was the standard US view that it was wrong that the industrialized countries (called the 'Annex 1' countries in the Framework Convention) should be required to commit themselves to control their ghg emissions while the developing countries ('non Annex 1' in the jargon) were not. The resolution, which was adopted by 95 votes with none against, is entirely consistent with C&C. It reads in part:

How Contraction & Convergence
conforms to the Byrd-Hagel Resolution

Over the years, the US has affirmed that:

1. A global solution to the global problem of climate change is needed.

2. The objective of the UNFCCC, the stabilisation of ghg concentration in the global atmosphere, inescapably requires ghg emissions to contract. [The graph shows them doing so between 2000 and 2100].

3. All countries must be involved in emissions control [2000–2200 in the graph].

4. A 'central organising principle' must be applied to determine which countries limit, and which countries cut, their emissions and by how much. (Initially the US said 'all countries will reduce ghg emissions by x% pro rata' [2050–2200 in the graph] This was later modified by the Byrd Hagel Resolution to combine 'Reductions' [controlled negative growth] with 'Limitations' [controlled positive growth] giving 'convergence' [2000–2050 in the graph].)

5. The 'commitments/entitlements' arising from this controlled contraction & convergence must be 100% tradable. Inter-emissions-budget-period borrowing must be allowed.

None of these requirements conflicts in any way with the basic C&C solution, namely, achieving equal per capita tradable entitlements for everyone on the planet by an agreed date under a predefined global cap. Can any other formula be developed that fits the US specification as well?

achieved by adopting the principle of per capita emissions rights that fully take into account the reality of population growth and the principle of differentiation.

Achievement of a safe limit to global greenhouse gas emissions can be achieved by reducing the emissions of Annex One while at the same time ensuring that there is controlled growth of future emissions from Non-Annex One countries, reflecting our legitimate right to sustainable economic growth. We strongly believe that this will take us along a path to responsible climate management that allows us to reach our goal of defining a mutually agreed point of convergence and sustainable development. Such a convergence, Mr. Chairman, must ensure that we maintain a global ceiling on emissions to prevent dangerous interference with the climate system.

When we look at time frames, we believe that insufficient commitment by Annex One countries will only result in delaying our influence on the climate system. If this course is maintained, then we will all suffer and the burden will be even greater for humanity in general. The burden for any future mitigation efforts on those of who have not been historically and currently responsible for creating the problem will be greater.
Mr. Chairman, we must focus our attention on the most appropriate, reasonable and acceptable time frame for action. There is an over-riding pre-requisite. The time frame cannot be too far away into the future if we are to avoid at all costs the dangers that global climate change poses. The current scientific evidence indicates that Africa faces decline in water resources, agricultural production and economic performance. It is therefore for this reason that we wish to register the seriousness with which we view the effective implementation of the Convention and future agreements emanating from it.

The Africa Group carried this position through to the end of COP-3 in December. It also planted the seed which led to the pro-Contraction & Convergence statement by the heads of government at the summit of the Non-Aligned-Movement (NAM) a year later in Durban, South Africa.

In Bonn in October at the final negotiations prior to COP-3 in Kyoto, I took the Song Jian statement to the American delegates and said, in effect, 'There you are. He says he'll meet you half way.' The delegates pointed out a group of people described as being from the Senate Armed Services Committee. Their line was abrupt. 'We won the Cold War. Contraction & Convergence is Communism.' 'Is that right?' I replied. 'But at least you get a capitalist management system with trading and with everyone in. The Chinese call it 'One-Planet-Two Systems'.' In truth the Chinese had only said that about Hong Kong but it was a good line.

COP-3, Kyoto, December

The Kyoto Protocol was tabled at COP-3 in an attempt to develop the Berlin Mandate. Under this, the industrialized countries were to make further emissions reductions after fulfilling the ones that they had declared they were 'aiming' to make when they signed the Framework Convention. As only the industrial countries were involved, the mandate was a 'sub-global' solution that left the tension over global participation unresolved. Moreover, in spite of the Africa Group's position, many developing countries wanted to keep it that way. They continued to resist making commitments themselves, and rejected a US bid to get them to make even 'voluntary' ones. This was not just because of the history of deep inequity and mistrust between them and the industrial countries. It was also because they were encouraged to do so by the Climate Action Network, a group of NGOs, which persuaded them to demand ever-deeper ghg emissions reductions from the developed country group over the next 50 years while pledging nothing in return themselves.

However, right at the end of the conference, during discussions about the international tradability of ghg emissions entitlements, an increasing number of countries began to see the logic behind the Africa Group's proposals for Contraction & Convergence. By definition, emissions trading cannot occur until the principle of property rights has been agreed and entitlements to the property have been assigned. Two hours after midnight on the last day, when the negotiations were already into injury time, the paragraph in the draft Kyoto Protocol relating to emissions trading came up for acceptance. The US reiterated its insistence on everyone's acceptance of emissions trading.

The governments of China and India, contrary to widespread expectations, did not reject the idea. Instead they responded by saying that they would agree to emissions trading if 'equitable allocations' of emissions entitlements were made to all countries on a per capita basis. After a long struggle, the Africa Group reiterated the call for Contraction & Convergence. The US reacted strongly, saying that this element was too much to handle in the middle of the night. The chairman, Raoul Estrada from Argentina, immediately suspended the meeting saying they were about to lose ten years' work. Daniel Reifsnyder, a good friend and a key player on the US delegation, stalked out in a fury, and told me that this mess was entirely my 'f****** fault'.

When the session resumed, Estrada read out a prepared text, now known as Article 17 to the Protocol. It instructed the technical bodies attached to the Convention Secretariat to work out how emissions trading should be carried out before COP-4 in Buenos Aires in November the following year. He then gavelled it through. No discussion. Total failure had been narrowly averted. The Americans called it a near-death experience.

Four months earlier Estrada, a seasoned diplomat, had told me that principles were usually made up to explain what had already happened in practice. Now, the reverse was required. If emissions trading is to be practised, property rights have to be created because you can't sell what you don't own. Creating such rights will require organising principles that synthesize everyone's interests and meet the goals of the Framework Convention. In other words, the Framework Convention requires a framework based on precaution and equity, as, without it, we have to fall back on *ad hoc* decisions, guesswork and attempts to fly by the seat of our pants.

Chapter 5

The Rising Tide of Support for C&C

Three years later, shortly before COP-6 in The Hague in November 2000, very little had changed internationally. People have not yet been able to resolve Article 17 of the Kyoto Protocol, so support for Contraction & Convergence has continued to rally steadily. Here are some significant examples:

May 1998 Prof Saifuddin Soz MP, Indian Environment Minister, in Kyoto: 'In any discussion [about Contraction & Convergence], the central point is entitlements—equitable per capita entitlements. At Kyoto we had stressed that any discussion on emissions trading ought to be framed in terms of per capita entitlements. Any trading can take place only after the emissions entitlements of the trading partners is defined and legally created—equitably of course. Historical emissions are iniquitous and cannot be the basis of entitlements. Entitlements will define the sharing of the atmosphere on an equitable basis which also brings together all the cooperative mechanisms in the Kyoto Protocol in a common framework.'

August 1998 The GLOBE International General Assembly in Cape Cod adopts a statement on the global management of climate change that incorporates Contraction and Convergence. It also urges the Non Aligned Movement of Nations (NAM) to persist in calling for equity at COP-4. Republican Senators and US Democratic signed the statement.

September 1998 The Non Aligned Movement Heads of Government Conference in Durban, South Africa, declares that 'Emission trading for implementation of (ghg reduction/limitation) commitments can only commence after issues relating to the principles, modalities, etc of such trading, including the initial allocations of emissions entitlements on an equitable basis to all countries, has been agreed upon by the Parties to the Framework Convention on Climate Change'.

September 1998 The GLOBE Southern Africa Network supports the Contraction & Convergence principles espoused by GLOBE and the Africa Group.

September 1998 The European Parliament adopts a resolution on climate change that calls for global constitutional principles for the long-term management of global climate change using Contraction & Convergence. The resolution, tabled by the Environment Committee, is intensely debated. It is finally adopted with a 90 per-cent majority in favour.

October 1998 The Environmental Justice Network Forum (EJNF) adopts an extensive resolution, 'committing itself to campaign in support of the Contraction & Convergence proposals that specifi-cally embody the principles of global equity and sustainability. This means that EJNF will advocate that the apportionment of future international greenhouse gas (ghg) emissions entitlements shall be the result of a deliberate convergence process to a point of equal per capita shares globally by a date to be negotiated by the United Nations Framework Convention on Climate Change.'

October 1998 Tony Blair, UK Prime Minister, writes: 'I agree that, in the fight against climate change [Contraction & Convergence] makes an important contribution to the debate on how we achieve long-term climate stability, taking account of the principles of equi-ty and sustainability.'

October 1998 Sir Robert May, UK Government Chief Scientist: 'Thank you for your letter of the 23rd April and for the information on 'Contraction & Convergence' policy and the efforts by GCI and GLOBE to build up global support for it. These matters are clearly of great importance and I would agree that this approach merits full consideration, including at the senior international political level, along with other ideas contributing to the development of a work-able global climate strategy'.

November 1998 John Porter, US Congressman, Chair GLOBE USA: 'Meaningful progress on confronting the challenge of climate change will only occur when countries from the North and the South are able to collaborate in issues of significant and sustainable development. The GLOBE Equity Protocol—Contraction &

Convergence—and its mechanism for financing sustainable development is the only proposal so far which is global, equitable and growth-oriented. It is precisely these issues that were endorsed at the GLOBE International General Assembly in Cape Cod, and form the thrust of our recently released (Nov 1998) paper, 'Solving Climate Change with Equity and Prosperity'.

April 1999 Svend Auken, Danish Environment Minister: 'The approach of "Contraction & Convergence" is precisely such an idea. It secures a regime that would allow all nations to join efforts to protect our global commons from being over-exploited, without the risk that any country would be deprived of its fair long-term share of the common environmental emission space. And it allows for consistent and efficient management of the global emissions that would enable us to strive for constraining global interference with the climate below fixed ceilings, such as the max. 2 degrees temperature rise, and the max. 550 ppmv CO_2-concentration, recommended by the European Council of Ministers.'

April 1999 Michael Meacher, the UK Minister of the Environment. 'But a much tighter and sharper framework of commitments is clearly now needed, and one that is focused on longer term emissions targets that are substantially lower. I note that Sir John Houghton, as chair of the IPCC, recently told the British Association for the Advancement of Science that global greenhouse gas emissions must be reduced by more than 60% in less than 100 years in order to stabilise their rising concentrations in the atmosphere. It is difficult to see that this can be achieved with universal global assent—the underlying basis of the Convention—without collective agreements that broadly reflect the principles of contraction & convergence. The growing evidence of sudden and highly damaging climatic events which we are already seeing world-wide only seem to emphasize the urgency of securing such a framework. I do believe that contraction and convergence provides an effective, equitable market-based framework within which Governments can co-operate to avert climate change'.

June 1999 Klaus Topfer, Director of the United Nations Environment Programme. 'Convergence—The review system of Kyoto mechanisms can ensure equity. Currently CO_2 emissions rights are allocated according to existing emissions patterns with a specified reduction percentage for various countries within a certain period of five years (2008-2012). The redistribution through the Kyoto Protocol could be continued until emissions rights are uniformly distributed on a per capita basis. This will be a critical element to ensure the poor also get rights to utilize the world's environment, or in this limited case, the assimilative capacity of the atmosphere, a global commons resource'.

January 2000 The Global Commons Network is established. It now consists of hundreds of eminent individuals, institutions and NGOs from all over the world who have signed the resolution printed at the end of this Briefing (which we would like you to sign as well).

February 2000 Ambassador Raul Estrada Oyuela, Former Chair of Kyoto Negotiations. 'Long before the end of the Framework Convention negotiation, the Global Commons Institute has presented a proposal on Contraction & Convergence, aimed to reach equality in emissions per capita. We all in this room know the GCI model where contraction is achieved after all governments, for precautionary reasons, collectively agree to be bound by a target of global GHG emissions, making it possible to calculate the diminishing amount of greenhouse gases that the world can release each year in the coming century, subject to annual scientific and political review. The convergence part of the proposal means that each year's global emissions budget gets shared out among the nations of the world so that every country converges on the same allocation per inhabitant by an agreed date. Countries unable to manage within their shares would be able to buy the unused parts of the allocations of other countries. The entitlement of rights transferred in this trading is legitimised by the per inhabitant criteria. Level of contraction and timing of convergence should be negotiated on the basis of the precautionary principle. Suggestions for emission reductions are well known and convergence should be achieved at medium term to satisfy legitimacy. I have read that the Chairman of IPCC's WGI, Sir John Houghton, has said that this is the "logical approach". Analysis of Contraction & Convergence in the IPCC Third Assessment Report is a must if equity is going to be taken into account in the report'.

June 2000 The International Federation of Red Cross and Red Crescent Societies affirm the need for a Contraction & Convergence agreement in their Disasters 2000 report.

June 2000 The Royal Commission on Environmental Pollution reports on energy and climate change to the British government. The third of its 87 key recommendations is one calling for an international Contraction & Convergence agreement with emissions trading. The report says that this has the best chance of securing the international consensus necessary to solve the world climate problem.

June 2000 Jan Pronk, the Chairman of COP-6, Netherlands Environment Minister, made a remarkably candid assessment of the ideas going forward to The Hague saying in effect that C&C is the most equitable, the cheapest and easiest and the most effective. The relevant part of the statement is worth reproducing in full. 'The debate about broadening participation of developing countries in the global effort to stabilize greenhouse concentrations in the atmosphere at sustainable levels has the tendency to focus first on the most advanced developing countries. Suggestions have been made for commitments for those developing countries in the period after 2012 in terms of increased energy or greenhouse gas efficiency. In other words: not an absolute cap, but a relative efficiency improvement in the production structure of developing countries. This strategy would imply that developing countries gradually start participating, as they achieve a certain level of economic development. That is a reasonable and realistic option. However, it can be argued that such gradual participation would only lead to a slow decline of global emissions, even if current industrialized countries would drastically decrease their emissions. As a result global average temperature increase would significantly exceed the 2 degrees centigrade limit that could be seen as the maximum tolerable for our planet. There are alternatives for this scenario. Some developing countries have argued for an allowance of equal emissions per capita. This would be the most equitable way to determine the contribution of countries to the global effort. If we agree to equal per capita emissions allowances for all countries by 2030 in such a way that global emissions allow us to stay below the 2 degrees global temperature increase (equivalent to about 450 ppmv CO_2), then the assigned amounts for Annex B countries would be drastically reduced. However, due to the fact that all countries would have assigned amounts, maximum use of global emissions trading would strongly reduce the cost of compliance. So, in such a scenario, industrialized countries would have to do more, but it would be cheaper and easier . . . '

2000 Sir John Houghton, the Chairman of the IPCC WG1, in *The Economist*'s 'The World in 2000'. 'Three widely accepted principles will govern the international agreements needed to meet the threat of climate change. The first is the Precautionary Principle, already clearly embedded in the UNFCCC agreed at the Earth Summit in Rio in 1992. This states that the existence of uncertainty should not preclude the taking an appropriate action. The reason for such action is simply stated as the stabilisation of the concentrations of greenhouse gases (such as CO_2) in the atmosphere in ways that allow for necessary economic development. The second principle is The Polluter Pays Principle, which implies the imposition of measures such as carbon taxes or carbon trading arrangements. The third is the principle of Equity, both intergenerational and international, which is the most difficult to apply. However a proposal by the Global Commons Institute that is being widely discussed applies these principles by allowing eventually for the allocation of carbon emissions to nations on an equal per capita basis while also allowing for emissions trading.'

Chapter 6

Framework versus Guesswork

The World Business Council for Sustainable Development (WBCSD) is a coalition of some of the richest and most powerful corporations on the planet. In its original form it was set up shortly before the Earth Summit in Rio in 1992, largely to take a role in arranging the proceedings. Its manifesto was a book, *Changing Course*, which acknowledged the problems of global over-consumption and the growing gap between the rich and poor, and called for solutions to be found.

At COP-4 in Kyoto in 1997, the WBCSD published a report, *Exploring Sustainable Development*, prepared under the direction of Ged Davis of Shell International. This tells 'stories of the future' in scenarios designed to help readers understand some of the challenges humanity can expect to meet in the years ahead and organise themselves to meet them. A lot of good strategic thought went into the report and the authors certainly stepped outside the box of conventional thought. The three scenarios were FROG, Geo-Polity and Jazz.

FROG stands for 'First Raise Our Growth', the attitude adopted by politicians who make remarks like 'If this country is able to grow, that will provide us with the resources we need for cleaning up the environment.' Mrs Thatcher's version of the tale of the Good Samaritan—to do good you must first be wealthy—represents the FROG position well. FROGs are not at all unhappy to continue handling problems within a political system characterised by hedging, disagreements and short-termist guesswork. In relation to climate change, many FROGs think that it is stupid to try to do anything at the moment because technologies will develop in the future which will make solutions much easier to adopt. They are hostile to the UNFCCC and the Kyoto Protocol because of the restrictions these would place on the availability of the fossil energy required for generating economic growth. In practice FROG amounts to the 'no-problem' position at COP-1.

Jazz reflects the concerns increasingly found in the business world about adverse trends in the environment and society. These concerns mean, for example, that despite the fact that the interests of a company's shareholders must come first, other stakeholders are consulted and environmental impact studies are carried out. In relation to the climate crisis, proponents of Jazz prefer to act tactically by increasing world energy efficiency at the lowest cost via 'flexible mechanisms' such as the Clean Development Mechanism, which allows companies to set off emissions increases in one country by reductions in another. Above all, they want to be free of government regulation. Corporate lobbyists have presented the 'flexibility' and 'spontaneity' of Jazz very effectively, but there is no escaping the fact that, because of the desire to be free from controls, the approach is generally cautious about the establishment of a global, legally binding framework for emissions reductions within the UN's Framework Convention. However as Jazzists definitely prefer tradable quotas to the eco-taxes proposed by economists, and recognise that quotas have to be limited if they are to work, they would not be fiercely opposed to the introduction of limits under C&C if they were sure they would be left alone to play their music afterwards. Jazz amounts to the 'no regrets', 'no regulations' position at COP-1.

Geo-Polity is short for 'Global Environmental Organisation Polity'. Supporters of this approach believe that the people of the world should act collectively to ensure all their futures. Although the 187 nations that signed the Framework Convention are in principle committed to geo-polity, their position is confused by the competing sub-global priorities of Jazz and FROG. The WBCSD authors, for example, tend to characterise geo-polity as anachronistic, inflexible and inefficient because of their distaste for centralised planning and control. This amounts to the 'no solutions without developing countries' position at COP-1. The US wanted this, but they also wanted Jazz.

The fact is, of course, that none of the actors in our 'universe of the ten thousand things', not even the multinational corporations or the United States itself, has the power to avert a climate crisis single-handedly or with sub-global agreements. We therefore need to work together to have any chance of doing so, and it is obvious that we have a much better chance of success if our global collaboration is based on an overall plan rather than relying on guidance coming from the market via the Invisible Hand. In other words, a framework for action gives us a chance to be effective. Guesswork is just guesswork. At the meta-level, C&C is the framework. It offers leadership by idea.

As the Kyoto Protocol is FROG- and Jazz-based, it is an inadequate, tactical, short-term, sub-global (Developed Countries, or 'Annex One' only) response to a long-term problem that obviously requires a strategic and collaborative, universal rights based geopolitical solution. The Protocol merely requires industrial countries to control their emissions of greenhouse gases to an arbitrary % of their 1990 level across a five-year 'budget-period', 2008-2012. The size of each country's control 'commitment' is shown in the table below. Note that some are 'reductions' while others are merely limitations' (see also box on page 81).

Who has promised what for their CO_2 emissions					
Country	CO_2 emissions in 1990, million tonnes	% of world emissions	Kyoto pledge	CO_2 per capita, tonnes	CO_2 per $ of GDP, grammes
United States	4,957	23	7% cut	19.83	246
Russia	2,389	11	No rise	16.13	1,071
Japan	1,173	5.4	6% cut	9.35	107
Germany	1,012	4.7	21% cut	12.79	169
UK	584	2.7	12.5% cut	10.04	161
Canada	457	2.1	6% cut	16.64	222
Italy	428	2.0	6.5% cut	7.51	107
Poland	414	1.9	6% cut	10.88	1,919
France	367	1.7	No rise	6.23	84
Australia	289	1.3	8% rise	17.12	268
Spain	261	1.2	15% rise	5.79	126
Romania	171	0.8	6% cut	7.37	1,220
Czech Rep.	170	0.8	8% cut	16.09	1,431
Netherlands	168	0.8	6% cut	11.21	161
Belgium	113	0.5	7.5% cut	11.18	196
Bulgaria	83	0.4	8% cut	9.24	1,092
Greece	82	0.4	25% rise	8.02	277
Hungary	72	0.3	6% cut	6.93	591
Sweden	61	0.3	4% rise	7.15	73
Austria	59	0.3	13% cut	7.70	102
Finland	53	0.2	No rise	10.81	109
Denmark	52	0.2	21% cut	10.12	110
Switzerland	44	0.2	8% cut	6.60	54
Portugal	42	0.2	27% rise	4.25	171
Norway	36	0.2	1% rise	8.36	84
Ireland	31	0.1	13% rise	8.76	187
New Zealand	26	0.1	No rise	7.59	160
Luxembourg	11	0.05	28% cut	29.76	299

Third World countries were not asked to make commitments to reduce their CO_2 emissions under the Kyoto Protocol. For comparison purposes, China had a CO_2 emission rate of 0.5 tonnes per person in 1990 and India a rate of 0.2 tonnes.

Each target was offered by a country itself, or in the case of the European Union, by the countries collectively. From the polluters' abatement-cost point of view, they were tentatively defensible. However, from the global damage-cost point of view, the figures the countries chose were entirely arbitrary. In fact, even if they were fully implemented, their effect would barely affect the rate at which greenhouse gases are accumulating in the atmosphere and the speed at which the global temperature is rising. What would one expect, as they were offered by entrenched climate debtors whose over-riding concern was to remain cost-competitive in world markets? This sort of approach can never work. What is needed instead is a set of arrangements that are globally effective in a way that is clear to all, and that is accepted by all. C&C offers this, although it offers no one all they want. Everybody will have to compromise. The Right will have to swallow a globally egalitarian 'pre-distribution' of emission rights, while the Left will have to go along with commercial dealing in these rights through international emissions trading. The South will accept that equitable entitlements are also commitments, and the North will accept that commitments can only be equitable entitlements.

Sub-global schemes, such as the collective arrangements made by the European Union for itself, may well be adopted on a much wider basis under C&C, but the distribution of the reductions within these groups—the jargon calls them 'bubbles'—would not form part of the UN negotiations.

In his book *Natural Capitalism*, Amory Lovins has popularised a type of hyper-Jazz economy based on treating the Earth's resources as natural capital. He accepts that natural capital is only available in limited amounts and, to his great credit, introduces the engaging and paradoxical notion of the economic value of negative consumption; such as miles not travelled (negamiles), watts of electricity not consumed (negawatts), etc. This is not just more efficient consumption. It is the benefit of real consumption avoided, something that is highly desirable for many reasons, resource conservation included.

Unfortunately, not even negative consumption can avoid the need for a precautionary global framework if the world is to avert the climate crisis. Lovins does not engage with this. He just says that climate change could be a 'faded memory in fifty years' if we stopped acting 'in irrationally inefficient ways'. Nor does he ask to how the limited amount of natural capital should be allocated, despite the fact that he has an excellent chapter on the failures of the free-market system. Adoption of C&C would have helped him to sort this out as it treats natural capital as a gift that, if it belongs to anyone, belongs to everyone in equal measure globally.

Quite often these days we find well-meaning, well-off people in debtor countries doing such things as putting photovoltaic panels on their roofs to generate electricity from the sun and cut their electricity bills. While this seems good if considered in isolation—in other words, in a sub-global context—it has to be recognized that their actions are, in effect, subsidized by people in the creditor countries who aren't consuming adequately, people who may not have had a filling meal for weeks. Moreover, without an overall framework that ensures that emission targets are met, installing photovoltaic panels in a system run by guesswork adds little to the prospect of long-term success. This is because such actions while good in themselves mustn't blunt the will to press for the radical changes necessary to correct the situation.

A larger-scale example of something that might be worthwhile at the sub-global level but is meaningless in the global picture, is the Sky Trust plan. Under this, the marginally restricted level of emissions that the US has allowed itself to release under the Kyoto Protocol would be auctioned off each year to oil, coal and gas companies, which would only be allowed to supply their customers with as much product as they had acquired emissions rights to release. The proceeds of the auction would then be shared out equally amongst the entire US population, giving them not only what would be, in effect, a citizen's income, but also extra cash to cover the higher prices that the higher fuel costs would cause.

The nice thing about Sky Trust is that the greater the restriction the US places on its emissions, the higher the price for the emissions rights at auction becomes, and the higher the income each citizen receives. Lower energy products become relatively cheaper than high-energy ones, encouraging people to switch their purchasing to

Kyoto's 'Flexible Mechanisms'

The Protocol is also drafted to include three so-called 'flexible mechanisms'; Joint Implementation (JI), Clean Development Mechanism (CDM), Emissions Trading(ET).

Despite the mixture of these creating effectively insuperable measurement problems, these are intended to allow as yet unspecified fractions of the Annex One commitments to be:

(1) 'jointly implemented' or bi-laterally bartered, within Annex One, (for example the US might acquire a fraction of the Russian commitment in exchange for modern emissions-avoiding technology going to Russia),

(2) 'traded' as emissions permits both in and priced by a newly created international market in these permits (at the moment this can be within the Annex One only) and

(3) partly achieved through a sort of 'mutual aid' scheme with the 'uncommitted' Developing Countries through an intended arrangement called the 'Clean Development Mechanism' (where an Industrial Country may seek to avoid its own emissions by funding projects in Developing Countries that are supposed to avoid emissions there in amounts equal to the declared shortfall in avoidance back home.

In addition, and again with almost insuperable measurement problems, the environmental and social pros and cons of tree planting (to 'capture' CO_2 back from the atmosphere) within and alongside these flexible mechanisms, are also being vigorously debated.

them as much as possible in an effort to save as much of their citizen's income as they can. It is neat, but only at the sub-global level. As soon as you bring the wider world in, the idea becomes less attractive. If, for example, the Sky Trust distribution proved so electorally popular that the US decided that it could accelerate its rate of emissions reduction and generate bigger payouts, the extent by which it could do so would be limited. This would be because large additional cuts would cause the price of emissions rights to rise, putting up the cost of energy to US industry, which would then find itself undercut by firms in countries with a much more leisurely contraction rate—or none at all. In short, Sky Trust has to be protected by an international framework if it is to work well.

The British government provides another example of the fuzzy thinking that is almost inevitable in the absence of a global frame-work. Early in 2000, John Prescott, the Deputy Prime Minister, announced that Britain would over-fulfil its Kyoto Protocol commit-ment to its EU partners. Instead of cutting its emissions by 12.5%, it would bring them down by 20%. The emission rights saved would be sold to help some other country meet its commitments and bring in millions of pounds. Excellent news. Or was it? At the national level, yes, but at the global level, definitely not. This is because Britain would be profiting not because it had overachieved a target set for it by the international community, which would be fair enough, but because it had under-committed itself when it volunteered to make the cuts. Unless a global framework is established, every participating country would learn from Britain's experience and under-commit itself in the hope of making a profit the next time around.

More importantly, even if Sky Trust went ahead and Britain made its 20% emissions cuts and sold the surplus, there's no guarantee that a runaway global warming would not develop. The combined cuts, plus those resulting from the installation of thousands of pho-tovoltaic panels, might easily not be enough to stabilize ghg levels in the atmosphere. How can any one guarantee to achieve that without an overall plan?

Is this analysis going to convince the corporate sector to join the coalition for equity and survival? I believe the answer is 'yes', as there is nowhere else to go. Businesspeople already prefer tradable quotas to eco-taxes and are gradually coming to understand that quotas created under a framework of C&C will be the most effective way of achieving the international solidarity and commercial flexibility on which global environmental security and, ultimately, all prosperity now depends. As we go to press with this booklet, major companies in the insurance and energy industries are considering coming on board. They have to decide whether the objectives of FROG and Jazz are achievable without this precautionary geo-political framework of C&C. My impression is that the wisest amongst them clearly know that their commercial aspirations will be progressively overwhelmed if randomness and drift continue.

In fact, the choice is for all of us. In my view it boils down either to sharing carbon entitlements between people globally, equitably and sustainably, or allowing a combination of naked economic and military power and climate disasters to work out some unscriptable allocation with incalculable costs. This is so because the only distribution of emissions rights that will be accepted voluntarily by the nations of the world is one that provides that every country should have the same per capita emissions rights by some future date. The moment you introduce additional factors into the primary 'pre-distribution', such as allowing colder countries the right to burn more fuel, the whole process would become a morass of competing claims for special circumstances. There would be 180 countries with 180 different arguments about equity and 180 reasons to inflate their shares. COPs could continue for the next 100 years without aggregating all the international rivalry, politicking and cross talk into a precautionary and consensual global ghg contraction agreement.

At the global level, any attempt to produce an agreement that uses additional factors besides population to determine the distribution of emissions rights would be deep folly. This is because even if it eventually succeeded in achieving a gradual global contraction of ghg emissions, the delay would be damaging, as gases would have continued to accumulate in the atmosphere throughout the negotiating process, causing higher world temperatures and rates of damage. A rough and ready agreement now is much better than the possibility of a rather more sophisticated one later on.

The challenge for NGOs is to recognise that many governments are accepting the fundamental principle of global equality under limits and that this will be a massive step forward in the general struggle for a more equitable and sustainable world. It is not good enough for NGOs to tell coal miners in West Virginia who already regard their jobs under threat that they, the NGOs, are going to 'smash the fossil fuel industry'. When miners hear this kind of rhetoric, they want to join with the opposing forces and smash heads.

The rule is, do no harm. We need to create conditions that make the transition to a state in which the level of ghgs in the atmosphere is starting to fall rapidly enough to be effective and smooth enough to be bearable. That is what frameworks are for. Alternatives have to be found. As the self-help groups say, if we are all honest about being victims and adopt simple rules for prevention and recovery, things can get better.

Special currency required for emissions trading

Several NGOs hold strong objections to international trading in greenhouse gas emissions rights. This is because they fear that any system that allows rich countries to consume their own entitlement and then buy more will allow such countries to avoid making serious cuts to their fossil fuel consumption. If this happened, it would perpetuate the energy-consumption gap between nations and thus, because of the CO_2/GDP lockstep, the income gap between the energy-intensive industrialised countries and the more labour-intensive primary-producing ones.

The NGOs might be right for the first few years after the implementation of C&C. If, for example, the rate at which it was agreed that global emissions should contract was over-cautious or if the world economy slowed down, then the price of permits to release more emissions might be so low that some countries simply bought more rather than investing in making themselves more energy-efficient. But if this happened, the problem would not be with C&C as a system but with the slow contraction rate. Moreover, the situation would not last and as, year by year, the number of emissions permits issued declined, sooner or later their price would rise until it made economic sense for real changes to be made in the industrialized countries.

In order to make C&C work fairly, however, it is vital to ensure that countries that do sell part of their emissions entitlements get good value for them. This will not happen under the present world monetary system. If, for example, the US buys extra emissions rights from India and pays for them in dollars, only a proportion of those dollars will actually go back to the US to buy American goods and services any time soon. The rest will circulate internationally as if they were a world currency financing national and international trade. This is one of the reasons that the US has been able to run a current account balance-of-payments deficit for many years: the rest of the world has been happy to use the US currency for trading amongst itself.

Every dollar, pound, Euro, yen or Swiss franc received in payment for goods, services or emissions rights that does not find its way back to the country which issued it almost immediately represents a subsidy to the economic system of the country from which it came. After all, the issuing country has had the benefit of the goods, services or rights it bought with the money but has not had to give anything up yet in return. This is grossly unfair. What it means in relation to C&C is that if the industrialized countries are allowed to buy extra emissions rights with money they have issued themselves, they will essentially be able to buy those rights at a substantial discount.

Richard Douthwaite proposed a solution to this problem in Schumacher Briefing No. 4, *The Ecology of Money*. He suggests the creation of a new world currency, the ebcu (this stands for Emissions-Backed Currency Unit) which would be issued by the body set up to handle the annual distribution of emissions permits under Contraction & Convergence. The new money would be distributed by being given to countries in proportion to their population at the same time as the first batch of emissions permits. This would be a once-only issue. No more ebcus would ever be given out.

The recipients would use their ebcus instead of national currencies for all their international trade, including emissions trading. This would immediately eliminate the economic advantage currently enjoyed by those countries with internationally acceptable currencies.

If the price of emissions rights in ebcus rose above a fixed rate, the issuing body would be prepared to sell additional permits. It would take the ebcus it received as a result of these sales out of circulation and the resulting tightness in the supply of the new currency would restrict the amount of international trade it was possible to carry on. This in turn would reduce the demand for fossil energy. In short, the system would fix the value of emissions rights in terms of ebcus and mean that the level of international economic activity was determined by the efficiency with which the world used fossil fuel.

National and local currencies would still exist, of course, and if the countries or regions in which these circulated were able to use fossil energy more efficiently than the global average by supplementing it with energy from renewable sources, they would be able to become more prosperous than less fossil-energy-efficient parts of the world. A fuller explanation of this system can be found in Douthwaite's book.

Chapter 7

Looking Back, Seeing Forward

The drama we are all caught up in is not fundamentally new. It is performed every time those running the money machine act on the basis that its defence is more important than anything else. The only new elements this time are the scale and urgency with which the action is being played out.

Being Zen involves letting go, and in its analysis, C&C lets go of money: there is not a single dollar involved. It only concerns itself with carbon and the people emitting the carbon, and attempts to organize them to solve the problem in a way so simple that a child could understand it. If the organising principles of C&C had been made more complicated, perhaps by introducing just a few all-too-loaded dollars, conflicting assumptions about these would have overwhelmed the simple rationale and the basic priority of equity and survival. It is money-led conflicts that are now being played out in the Kyoto Protocol negotiations. It wasn't the paltry level of the emissions reductions promised by the industrial countries in the Protocol that constituted 'the tragedy and farce' denounced by Greenpeace, it was the dither and drift that arose from the desire to pursue the growth illusion.

The battle lines are very clear. You either accept that the reduction of greenhouse gas emissions is more important than the pursuit of economic growth, or you don't. If you do, then it's not too hard to accept that you need a framework within which the reduction can be brought about. As we have said, we are not against the growth of economic opportunity, but this cannot mean a continuation of expansion and divergence. That process contracts opportunities as it concentrates incomes and wealth into fewer and fewer hands. Nor must opportunities be created at the expense of ruining the planet. Even the act of considering possible trade-offs—a few more emissions for the sake of this or that economic advantage—is not only wrong-headed, it is wrong.

Now is the time to act. By 'now' I mean the period (if it has not passed already) during which we still have the choice of whether or not to stabilize the climate by cutting emissions within an effective framework that guarantees the result. As the Devastating Trends graph in the colour section after page 32 shows, the rate of climate change is accelerating. This means that if we do not positively choose to use a framework 'now', we are choosing guesswork by default and will almost certainly be plunged into a rapid, unstoppable change in the world's climate. Many climate scientists think that a runaway greenhouse effect is possible and in the statement I mentioned earlier, Stephen Hawking even suggested that the Earth could become like Venus, where 90% of the atmosphere is made up of CO_2 and midday temperatures reach five times that of boiling water. Essentially, he was saying that 'now' was over and we should begin planning to leave the planet eventually. As my frail but witty landlady said when I told her this, 'Oh dear, where shall we go? Shall I pack?'

Since we don't know when 'now' ends, we cannot tell how close we are to it. The only information might come when it's too late. Think of sneezing. A sneeze starts with an intake of breath and ends with an explosion. Can you feel one coming? Stephen Hawking obviously can. And it is unstoppable long before it actually happens.

Precautionary behaviour means avoiding risks we need not run. The Jazz economy works quite the other way. It links high risks with high rewards and, simply by being on the planet while it is operating, we have all put our stakes down. Some of us will win in the short-term, but we will all lose in the long term. When climate damage exceeds the world's GDP—perhaps around 2050—the game's over. So our generation carries the responsibility of acting while there is still time to do so. Dancing in the dark to Jazz will end with the dawning of a structure that includes the following points.

• A mandate for Contraction & Convergence is agreed by the nations that signed the Framework Convention to supersede the Kyoto Protocol at the appropriate moment.

• A target atmospheric concentration level of 400 parts of CO_2 per million is set, with convergence on a per capita emissions entitlement consistent with this, to be completed by 2030. The annual reduction rate in emissions and the final level of emissions at convergence would be subject to regular review to ensure the target is reached.

• A global reserve fund of emissions-backed currency units (ebcus) is established.

• The ebcus in the fund are distributed in proportion to each country's population when the C&C agreement is ratified and emissions rights are issued in accordance with it. This allows a start to trading ebcus for emission rights.

The 'pre-distribution' of ebcus would allow countries to fund clean technology such as photovoltaics, solar hydrogen energy, wind and wave power, etc. It would also allow countries to clear their international debts immediately since the disappointing progress made by Jubilee 2000 so far makes it seem unlikely that many will be cancelled.

As I write, it is only five weeks until COP-6 opens and a huge amount of political energy will be expended trying to make the US ratify the Kyoto Protocol. Will it? The fact that I believe the answer to this is 'no' is much less important than the fact that I believe it is the wrong question, for the reasons given in the box. What is important is the need for the C&C framework to be mandated.

* * * * *

When GCI began its work ten years ago, the Gulf War started too, and instead of human thought and energy going into ways of decreasing dependency on fossil fuels, it went instead into ensuring the continuity of supplies because of the FROG, Jazz and Geo-Political priorities of the people who sent their forces to war.

Although these priorities are still held tenaciously, new elements have come into play. The trebling of the price of oil in the past two years has happened largely because the world's oil is running out and 38% of the remaining reserves are now in the hands of the five major OPEC countries in the Middle East, a fact that gives them a lot of muscle in the market. Within ten years, these five countries will control 50% of the world's oil, and supplies will have started to fall because, even if the producers wanted to do so, it just won't be there to extract.

Will the US ratify the Kyoto Protocol?

There are four answers to this question: 'yes', 'no', 'maybe' and 'it depends on when these conditions arise'.

If every country were to agree to a system of emissions control and limitation before the date of the next US election as this book comes off the press, and this system placed no restrictions on the amount of emissions trading that could occur, we would have achieved 'globality' so the answer is 'yes'. This might still be true after 2002 as well. It depends on which party wins the White House and which party captures the Senate.

If only the industrial countries were pledged to take part and quantitative limits were placed on the amount of emissions they could trade, the answer is 'no'.

If limits are set on the amount of emissions trading and major developing countries gave worthwhile commitments on the level of their future emissions, the answer is 'maybe'.

In any case, asking whether the US will ratify the Kyoto Protocol is the wrong question. A better question would be 'If the US ratifies the Protocol, will anything change?' My fear is that it could prove worse than useless. This is because the cut it proposes is so inadequate that they would not stop the acceleration in the rate at which the Earth's temperature is rising, let alone stabilise the temperature itself. The danger is that this will not get through to the public, who will be quite happy to accept that something is at last being done.

This is the real oil crisis and, like global warming, it is a dilemma of framework versus guesswork. Indeed, we find the same four noes here too.

The first is 'no problem', the attitude expressed by those who refuse to believe that oil stocks are running down. This is just as dishonest and dangerous as denying the reality of climate changes because time that should have been used for strategic planning is wasted on futile arguments.

The second is 'no-regrets'—as before, this is limiting one's response to doing things which it makes sense to do anyway. For example, the International Energy Agency (the energy arm of the OECD) is currently advising its member nations to reduce their dependence on oil by diversifying geographical sources of supply, exploring other energy technologies and curbing demand by increasing energy efficiency. This is the Jazz position.

The third is the issue of 'no leadership'. The UK provides a good example of the inadequacy of Jazz-based management. The British government earns revenue from a high but quite arbitrary tax on oil that it hopes will curb demand. The fuel rioters demand that the tax is reduced while the environmentalists demand that it goes up. The rioters blame the government while the government blames OPEC and then asks the environmentalists to oppose the rioters, while the environmentalists blame everybody for wanting to consume the oil as it causes climate change. What all these arguments lack is a shared understanding of oil depletion, and of the devastating trends of expansion, divergence and climate change. Consequently there is no possibility of leadership, let alone a solution, because not enough people have yet grasped that a global framework is needed if these twin crises are to be brought under control.

This obviously creates the fourth 'no', namely 'no solutions without developing countries'. All-inclusive solutions are needed because the energy problem, like the climate problem, is global. And without a suitable worldwide framework that everyone accepts, neither crisis will go away.

Please read the letter opposite, a shorter version of which was published in The Independent (UK), 24th December 1999. We invite you to add your name to the list of signatories. One way of doing this on the GCI website (see Resources on page 94); or you can cut out the page and send to your political representative. If you send such a letter by post, please let GCI know and we will add your name to the online database.

Open Letter to World Leaders

Dear Sir,

The debts that the wealthy countries have recently forgiven their poorer neighbours are as nothing in comparison with the amount that these countries already owe the rest of the world for the increased global warming they have caused and are still causing. Inevitably there are links between this and the rising frequency and severity of storms, floods, droughts and the damage these are causing in many places across the world.

While debts worth roughly $3 billion have just been conditionally written off by the UK, the cost of the infra-structural damage done by the recent floods in Venezuela alone has been put at $10 billion. In addition, tens of thousands of lives have been lost there. Is anybody brave enough to put a monetary value on these?

Moreover, the greenhouse gases the energy-intensive countries have discharged into the atmosphere in the past two centuries will stay potentially even beyond the new century, causing death and destruction year after year. The debt relief, on the other hand, is a one-off event. Fifty-six countries were affected by severe floods and at least 45 by drought during 1998, the most recent year for which figures are available. In China, the worst floods for 44 years displaced 56 million people in the Yangtze basin and destroyed almost five per cent of the country's output for the year, for which climate change was one of the causes. In Bangladesh, an unusually long and severe monsoon flooded two-thirds of the country for over a month and left 21 million people homeless.

Paul Epstein of Harvard Medical School has estimated that in the first eleven months of 1998, weather-related losses totalled $89billion and that 32,000 people died and 300 million were displaced from their homes. This was more than the total losses experienced throughout the 1980s, he said. The rate of destruction will accelerate because greenhouse gases are still being added to the atmosphere at perhaps five times the rate that natural systems can remove them. By 2050, annual losses could theoretically amount to anywhere between 12 per cent and 130 percent of the gross world product. In other words, more than the total amount the world produces that year could be destroyed and life as we know it could collapse. For the industrialized countries, the damage could be anywhere between 0.6 per cent and 17 per cent of their annual output, and for the rest of the world, between 25 per cent and 250 per cent.

Michael Meacher, the UK Environment Minister, has recognised this. He recently told the Royal Geological Society that, "the future of our planet, our civilisation and our survival as a human species... may well depend on [our responding to the climate crisis by] fusing the disciplines of politics and science within a single coherent system."

'Contraction & Convergence' is such a system. As Sir John Houghton, Chair of the Intergovernmental Panel on Climate Change (IPCC) recently told the British Association for the Advancement of Science, global greenhouse emissions need to be reduced by at least 60% in less than a hundred years.

When governments agree to be bound by such a target, the diminishing amount of carbon dioxide and the other greenhouse gases that the world could release while staying within the target can be calculated for each year in the coming century. This is the contraction part of the process.

The convergence part is that each year's tranche of this global emissions budget gets shared out among the nations of the world in a way that ensures that every country converges on the same allocation per inhabitant by, say, 2030, the date Sir John suggested. Countries unable to manage within their allocations would, within limits, be able to buy the unused parts of the allocations of other, more frugal, countries.

Sales of unused allocations would give the countries of the South the income to purchase or develop zero-emission ways of meeting their needs. The countries of the North would benefit from the export markets this restructuring would create. And the whole world would benefit by the slowing the rate at which damage was being done.

Because 'Contraction & Convergence' provides an effective, equitable and efficient framework within which governments can work to avert climate change, even some progressive fossil fuel producers have now begun to demonstrate a positive interest in the concept. Consequently, as Jubilee 2000 and Seattle have shown, governments and powerful interests are helped to change by coherent coordinated pressure from civil society.

Yours sincerely

References

Chapter 1
1. A summary of the results is available at:
http://www.meto.govt.uk/sec5/CR_div/Brochure98/index.html
2. Background Brief, Conference of the Parties 4, UN Framework
Convention on Climate Change, Buenos Aires, November 2, 1998.
3. E.G. Nisbet, *Leaving Eden: To protect and manage the Earth*,
Cambridge University Press, Cambridge, 1991, pp.65-6.
4. E. Nisbet, 'Climate change and methane', *Nature*, Vol. 347,
September 1990, p.23.
5. Hansen, James, Sato M., Ruedy R., Lacis A. and Oinas V., 'Global
Warming in the Twenty-first Century: an Alternative Scenario',
Proceedings of the National Academy of Science, June 2000. A summary of this paper can be found at:
<www.giss.nasa.gov/research/impacts/altscenario/>
6. *Beyond Growth*, Beacon Press, Boston, 1996.
7. Estimates of national income, corrected for such things as pollution and the use of natural resources including fossil fuel as if they
were income rather than a capital stock, have been prepared for
many countries. These are called Indices of Sustainable Economic
Welfare. Of the thirteen studies mentioned in Richard Douthwaite's
The Growth Illusion (Green Books, 2000) only two revealed
economies in which the growth process was not destroying more
resources than it created on a sustainable basis.
8. *The Management of Greed*, Resource Use Institute, Edinburgh,
1997.

Chapter 3
1. Paper delivered at a symposium, 'Critical Issues in the
Economics of Climate Change', Paris, 1996, and available from
IPIECA (International Petroleum Industry Environmental
Conservation Association), London.

Resources

GCI Resources

Global Commons Institute (GCI)
e-mail: aubrey@gci.org.uk www.gci.org.uk

Technical support, information concerning 'Contraction & Convergence' (C&C) and model (CCOptions) at: www.gci.org.uk

Global Commons Network (GCN)
Please join GCN by registering your political support for C&C at:
www.gci.org.uk/indlet.html

With GCN membership you receive updates and have access to:
www.igc.topica.com/lists/GCN/prefs/info.html

Full C&C support, advocacy, and reference list at:
www.gci.org.uk/Refs/C&CRefs3.pdf

Other Resource Websites

United Nations Framework Convention on Climate Change
www.unfccc.de

Intergovernmental Panel on Climate Change
www.ipcc.ch/

National Ocean Atmosphere Administration US
www.ngdc.noaa.gov/

Charter 99
www.charter99.org

Centre for Science and Environment India
www.cseindia.org

Christian Aid—Climate Debt Equity and Survival
www.christian-aid.uk/f_reports.htm

Institute for Global Dialogue—*December 1998*
www.igd.org.za/publications/global_dialogue/official_view/climate.html

World Rainforest Movement—2000
www.wrm.org.uy/english/plantations/material/carbonshop.htm

Population International—1994
www.cnie.org/pop/CO2/intro.htm

SCHUMACHER BRIEFINGS

The Schumacher Society is now extending its outreach with the Schumacher Briefings—carefully researched, clearly written 20,000-word booklets on key aspects of sustainable development, to be published three times a year. They offer readers:

• background information and an overview of the issue concerned
• an understanding of the state of play in the UK and elsewhere
• best practice examples of relevance for the issue under discussion
• an overview of policy implications and implementation.

The first Briefings are as follows:

No 1: Transforming Economic Life: A Millennial Challenge
by James Robertson, published in co-operation with the New Economics Foundation. Chapters include Transforming the System; A Common Pattern; Sharing the Value of Common Resources; Money and Finance; and The Global Economy.

No 2: Creating Sustainable Cities by Herbert Girardet. Shows how cities can dramatically reduce their consumption of resources and energy, and at the same time greatly improve the quality of life of their citizens. Chapters include Urban Sustainability, Cities and their Ecological Footprint, The Metabolism of Cities, Prospects for Urban Farming, Smart Cities and Urban Best Practice.

No 3: The Ecology of Health by Robin Stott. This Briefing is concerned with how environmental conditions affect the state of our health; how through new processes of participation we can regain control of what affects our health, and the kinds of policies that are needed to ensure good health for ourselves and our families.

No 4: The Ecology of Money by Richard Douthwaite. Explains why money has different effects according to its origins and purposes. Was it created to make profits for a commercial bank, or issued by government as a form of taxation? Or was it created by users themselves purely to facilitate their trade? This Briefing shows that it will be impossible to build a just and sustainable world until money creation is democratized.

Future Briefings will deal with issues such as education, food and farming, globalization, local development, environmental ethics, energy policy, alternatives to genetic engineering and green technology. The Briefings are being published by Green Books on behalf of the Schumacher Society. To take out a subscription, or for further details, please contact the Schumacher Society office (see page 96)

THE SCHUMACHER SOCIETY
Promoting Human-Scale Development

The Society was founded in 1978 after the death of economist and philosopher E. F. Schumacher, author of seminal books such as *Small is Beautiful*, *Good Work* and *A Guide for the Perplexed*. His sought to explain that the gigantism of modern economic and technological systems diminishes the well-being of individuals and communities, and the health of nature. His works has significantly influenced the thinking of our time.

The aim of the Schumacher Society is to:

• help assure that ecological issues are approached, and solutions devised, as if people matter, emphasising appropriate scale in human affairs;

• emphasize that humanity can't do things in isolation. Long-term thinking and action, and connectedness to other life forms, are crucial;

• stress holistic values, and the importance of a profound understanding of the subtle human qualities that transcend our material existence.

At the heart of the Society's work are the Schumacher Lectures, held in Bristol every year since 1978, and now also in Liverpool and Manchester. Our distinguished speakers, from all over the world, have included Amory Lovins, Herman Daly, Petra Kelly, Jonathon Porritt, James Lovelock, Wangari Maathai, Matthew Fox, Ivan Illich, Fritjof Capra, Arne Naess, Maneka Gandhi, James Robertson and Vandana Shiva.

Tangible expressions of our efforts over the last 20 years are: the Schumacher Lectures; Resurgence Magazine; Green Books publishing house; Schumacher College at Dartington, and the Small School at Hartland, Devon. The Society, a non-profit making company, is based in Bristol and London. We receive charitable donations through the Environmental Research Association in Hartland, Devon. Schumacher Society Members receive:

• a free lecture ticket for either Bristol, Liverpool or Manchester
• the Schumacher Newsletter
• the catalogue of the Schumacher Book Service
• information about Schumacher College Courses
• a list of other members in your area, on application

The Schumacher Society, The CREATE Environment Centre,
Smeaton Road, Bristol BS1 6XN Tel/Fax: 0117 903 1081
<schumacher@gn.apc.org> <www.oneworld.org/schumachersoc>

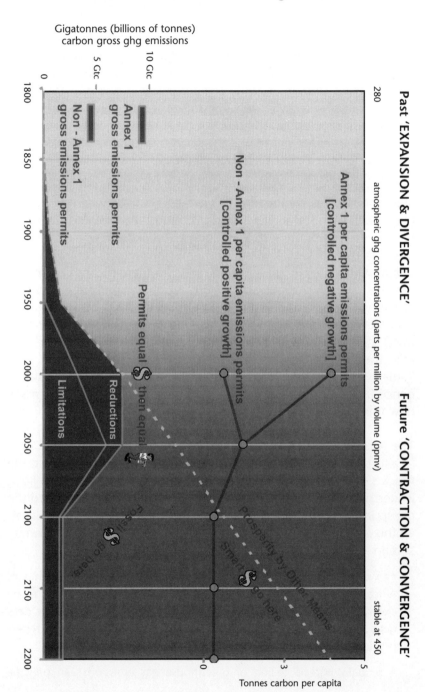

Gigatonnes (billions of tonnes)
carbon gross ghg emissions

10 Gtc

5 Gtc

0

Annex 1
gross emissions permits

Non - Annex 1
gross emissions permits

Annex 1 per capita emissions permits
[controlled negative growth]

Non - Annex 1 per capita emissions permits
[controlled positive growth]

Permits equal 🖐 then equal

Reductions

Limitations

Fossil oil on tap

Smart 🖐 go here

Prosperity by Other Means

1800 1850 1900 1950 2000 2050 2100 2150 2200

Past 'EXPANSION & DIVERGENCE'   Future 'CONTRACTION & CONVERGENCE'

280

atmospheric ghg concentrations (parts per million by volume (ppmv)

stable at 450

0   3   5

Tonnes carbon per capita

'Now, therefore, be it Resolved that: -

(1) The United States should not be a signatory to any protocol to, or other agreement regarding, the United Nations Framework Convention on Climate Change of 1992, at negotiations in Kyoto in December 1997, or thereafter, which would mandate new commitments to limit or reduce greenhouse gas emissions for the Annex I Parties, unless the protocol or other agreement also mandates new specific scheduled commitments to limit or reduce greenhouse gas emissions for Developing Country Parties within the same compliance period.'

Note the two key distinctions this makes, firstly between the Annex One Parties and the Developing Country Parties and secondly between a commitment to 'limit' ghg emissions and one to 'reduce' them. In this context, limiting ghg emissions means controlling the rate at which they increase, while reducing them means controlling the rate at which they are actually cut back. If we put these concepts together, the paragraph can only translate into a process of formal Contraction & Convergence. Annex One Parties will reduce (or contract) their ghg emissions, while the Developing Country Parties will limit their ghg emissions (so as to converge with the Annex One Parties). Technically, not just rhetorically, there has to be a 'convergence factor' to do this. It won't happen by accident. You can see how this might work on the graph on page 65.

The Africa Group respond

At a further set of inter-sessional negotiations in Bonn in August, the Africa Group of Nations took a clear initiative under the brilliant leadership of Rungano Karimanzira of Zimbabwe. She convened the group in an intense strategy session and then defined and presented this statement of Contraction & Convergence at the final plenary session.

As we negotiate the reduction of greenhouse gases, the countries of Africa believe that there should be certain principles that need to be clearly defined. There must be limits on all greenhouse gases if the danger to our climate is to be averted. The IPCC scientific assessment report provides us with the basis for global consensus on such limits.

A globally agreed ceiling of greenhouse gas emissions can only be